s are to be returned on or before
the last date below

16. MAR

PARLIAMENT
AND ITS SOVEREIGNTY

BY THE SAME AUTHOR

Death of a Gentleman
Fossett's Memory
Letters to a Sister
Can Parliament Survive?
A Study of George Orwell
Along the Road to Frome
Eton
The Homicide Act
The Oxford Union
Newman and the Modern World
The Mind of Chesterton
etc.

Parliament
and its Sovereignty

CHRISTOPHER
HOLLIS

HOLLIS & CARTER
LONDON SYDNEY
TORONTO

© Christopher Hollis 1973
ISBN 0 370 01358 1
Printed and bound in Great Britain for
Hollis & Carter Ltd
an associate company of The Bodley Head Ltd
9 Bow Street, London WC2E 7AL
by Richard Clay (The Chaucer Press) Ltd
Bungay, Suffolk
Set in Monotype Imprint
First published 1973

CONTENTS

CONTENTS

V

LEGISLATION, DIRECT AND DELEGATED 121

VI

FINANCE 137

VII

PARLIAMENT AND FOREIGN AFFAIRS 151

VIII

THE GROWTH OF PARLIAMENTARY DEMOCRACY 155

IX

PARLIAMENT AND THE CROWN 171

X

THE FUTURE OF SOVEREIGNTY 175

PREFACE

Accounts of the working of Parliament, both by constitutional historians and in the reminiscences of Members of Parliament, ex-Members and Parliamentary journalists, are very numerous. There would be no great point in adding one more to their number. But the proposals made for British entry into the European Community have demanded of Parliament a uniquely important and revolutionary decision. It is no part of the business of this book to argue whether such a decision is good or bad, whether entry is desirable or undesirable, though I do confess in a passing sentence in this book's closing chapter that, if I were still a Member of Parliament, I would have given my vote in favour of entry. My purpose, however, is not so much to argue the one side or the other as to assess the effectiveness of Parliamentary sovereignty as we have lately known it and to make clear how large, for better or for worse, is the revolution that is being made.

Ever since 1688 we have lived under Parliamentary sovereignty. That is to say, Parliament has been our absolute sovereign. Whatever authority any other bodies may have had over us, they have had by the delegation of Parliament—a delegation of powers which it was always open to Parliament to revoke. What Parliament—that is, the King or Queen in Parliament—has declared to be the law has been the law, and there has been no appeal against it. If Parliament decreed, it has been said—perhaps with some exaggeration—that the King should be executed, he would have no alternative but to give his royal assent. The judges under the British system have had no authority as against Parliament. All that they can do is to declare what is the law, what Parliament has decreed, and, if Parliament does not like what they say, it can always pass a further law to correct them. Now, by the legislation for entry into the

Community, Parliament has been asked to consent, and has consented, to accept the Treaties of Rome and of Brussels, by which the law that is to be imposed in Britain is on certain points decreed not by the British Parliament but by an entirely extra-British policy. We not only accept from an extra-British body the regulations which it has already made, but also give to it an unlimited power to make further regulations in the future. It may be that for the moment the ordinary British citizen will not encounter much difference in his private life. In a vital matter—such as the exchange rate—states will not be very obedient to regulations that are inconvenient to them: if Britain should reject M. Pompidou's demand that we cease floating the pound before our entry into the Community, perhaps nothing very much will happen, and the Community will prove to be in practice little more than a conventional alliance—a *Europe des patries*. After all, in the last resort, sovereignty is not a matter of paper constitutions or of sentiment but of force. Europe will only be fully a single state when there is a European army and a European police force which can enforce its commands on recalcitrant members or recalcitrant individuals, and that day is still far distant.

Yet the obligations that we are accepting are clear and unprecedented, as was shown by the Report of the House of Commons' Select Committee on Procedure on August 9, 1972. It would not be very decent to proceed on the assumption that we are not going to perform them. Not only do we accept the regulations which the Community has issued but, as I say, we also accept in anticipation those which it may issue in the future. Our judges will be under obligation to enforce these regulations in our courts, with the guidance of the European Court which will have the ultimate and overriding interpretation of the Treaties. The courts will no longer be, as they have been for the last three hundred years, what Lord Denning has called 'subservient' to Parliament. There will be for the first time a distinction between 'Municipal' and 'Community' law— laws which are not and which are affected by Community decisions—and the courts may have to decide that an act of the British Parliament is invalid if it is inconsistent with overriding Community law. The British civil service will necessarily change its pattern. Hitherto the civil servant has been content merely to serve his minister, who derives his authority from Parliament. Now legal authorities within the civil service will have to decide and to advise whether the minister's policy, though itself supported by Parliament, is legal. The obligations which we accept under the Treaties are not like the obligations of numerous previous treaties, for a definite, limited period. They are obligations in perpetuity, and after a short period it is very likely that our economy will be so intimately integrated with those of our Continental partners that it will no longer be possible to unscramble the egg even if we should wish to do so. It is true that the Union with Ireland of 1800 was intended to be in perpetuity and there was no provision for its possible repeal: nevertheless it was eventually repealed. There were, however, endless financial complications in effecting the repeal, and the contribution of Ireland to the British economy was very trivial in comparison with that of our partners to the finance of the European Community.

Of course it is said—and truly—that we will not be merely subjects of the European Community: we will be members of it and able to play our part in the shaping of its policies. It is complained, though, that those policies are shaped not by elected democratic representatives but by bureaucrats. This is for the moment true, but there is no doubt at all that before long there will be established something of the nature of a European Parliamentary Assembly through which a democratic control over the bureaucrats will be exercised; the exact form of that Assembly has not yet been settled. But, however democratic and just in its exercise of sovereignty this European Assembly may be, it will not be the traditional British Parliament. The Report of the Select Committee is only able to recommend that the House be kept informed of Community regulations; it will not have the power to amend them. Nor is it mere national prejudice that makes critics a little alarmed that ultimate sovereignty will pass to the Community from the British Parliament. Although it is true that the Continental countries all have parliaments and may in a loose way be called democracies, yet their parliaments profoundly differ from ours. Our parliament is, as we say, absolutely sovereign. Theirs all operate under written constitutions. Special procedures—plebiscites, special majorities or the like—are required to change their constitutions. Votes which do not satisfy those conditions are invalid. If they pass laws which offend the constitutions, those laws can be challenged in the courts. The parliaments of the European countries and any Parliament of Europe that may be established are and will be profoundly different institutions from the British Parliament. For better or for worse we will pass for the first time in our history under a constitution that is not only not purely British but under a Parliament with limited powers and a written constitution.

CHRISTOPHER HOLLIS
October 1972

I

THE ORGANISATION OF PARLIAMENT

1

The Sovereignty of Parliament

Parliament, it is sometimes said, can do anything except make a man a woman. Unlike other countries, which have federal constitutions or a written constitution buttressed by a Bill of Rights, in Great Britain the sovereignty of Parliament is absolute: or at any rate was so prior to the legislation imposed by the Treaties of Rome and Brussels which legitimised our entry into the European Community, the effect of which will be considered in a later chapter in this book. Parliament of course does not mean, as many people assume, merely the House of Commons. It means the King or Queen in Parliament: the House of Lords and the House of Commons passing legislation which is only on the Statute Book when it has received the royal assent. There has been no example, however, since 1707, of the Sovereign refusing the royal assent to a bill passed by Parliament. Further, the Parliament Act of 1911 gave the House of Commons the right, after three passages, to demand the royal assent for a bill which the Lords have not accepted; and the Parliament Act of 1949 modified this rule to two passages. And finally, ever since 1407, in Henry IV's time, the House of Commons has been conceded the right to initiate all monetary grants and the Lords have no right to amend finance bills. Therefore it follows that it is to the House of Commons that the Government owes its loyalty. It will resign if it loses the confidence of the Commons. It will not resign if defeated in the Lords.

2
The Two-Party System

It is the universal experience that a legislative assembly of any size is only manageable if its members accept a certain party organisation. Britain is in no way peculiar in having parties. Where it is peculiar is in having, generally and predominantly, only two parties. In the United States, it is true, there are also only two parties of importance, but parties in American politics have so entirely different a meaning from that in this country that there is no parallel between them. In America the President is elected separately from Congress. Congress even if it be of the same party as the President (as it by no means always is) has no obligation to sustain the President on details of legislation. There is in America no party discipline. Members of a party are under no obligation to vote the same way. As M. Duverger puts it (*Political Parties*, 1964, p. 210), they 'are founded on no ideological or social basis. They are simply organisations for the conquest of political office'. On the Continent legislators always organise themselves into a number of parties. In Britain alone have they tended to a two-party system. Hastings in his *Parliament House* suggests that this is to some extent due to architectural history. Parliament in the Middle Ages had no regular meeting-house; its members had to follow the King about wherever he might be. It was only in Edward VI's time that the Commons were given a regular home in what had previously been St. Stephen's Chapel in the Palace of Westminster, and it was because that chapel was narrow and rectangular that the Members sat on two rows of benches facing each other as in choir stalls, rather than in a hemicycle as in Continental countries.

It is true that this architectural accident did not mean

that Members from the first grouped themselves into two parties. We find something like party organisation in the seventeenth century at the time of the challenge to Charles I in the Civil War, in Charles II's time in the controversy over the exclusion of James, Duke of York, from the succession, and at the revolution of 1688. It would be an exaggeration to say that in these times we had party government. Once the religious issue was raised, opinion as between Charles and his opponents was, even in Parliament, much more closely balanced than is often thought. The Grand Remonstrance was only carried by 11 votes, by 159 to 148, in a House of 558. In the Commons 175 Members supported Charles when the war came. In the Lords he had 110 supporters to 30 opponents. Charles II played his hand much too astutely and subtly to allow the emergence of clear-cut issues. William III, when he came to the throne, at first tried to rule with a combination of Whig and Tory ministers. With the Hanoverian succession the Tories, tainted as they were with Jacobitism, were reduced to an insignificant rump. The eighteenth century did not give us a party system in any sense in which we use the word today. There were not two parties—Whigs and Tories—ranged against one another, the one in power, the other in opposition and anxious to get into power. All those who held power in the eighteenth century called themselves Whigs; the controversies were controversies between rival personal factions, not divided from one another by any permanent difference of principle. Parliament was supreme, but a Parliament built out of factions. It is curious that the eighteenth century, the first century of full Parliamentary domination, was also a century singularly barren of any constitutional innovation. Once Triennial Parliaments had been abolished, and the Septennial Act passed (see p. 58), and the Union with Scotland achieved, there was no serious demand for any further change. The demands for reform were half-hearted and quite unsuccessful.

Fox indeed at the end of the century challenged Pitt over the French revolutionary war but his supporters were so few that we cannot call the duel between these two an exercise in party government. The party system in anything like its modern form first made its appearance in the controversies over the Reform Bill. There we really had two parties arrayed against one another—the Whigs in favour of reform and the Tories against it—and after the Reform Bill under Melbourne and Peel the two parties were prepared to take it turn and turn about to be in power. But the two-party system, if it made its appearance in the 1830s, was disrupted again in the 1840s. Peel, by repealing the Corn Laws, destroyed the unity of the Tory party (the Conservative party as it had by then come to be called), and over the next decade there were three parties —the Liberals, the Peelites and the Protectionists. The consequence was a constant shifting of allegiance and a series of coalition governments. Trollope's Lord Plantagenet Palliser was able, so Trollope tells us, to sit for twelve years in the House of Commons without deciding to which party he belonged. Those who strongly dislike the notion of party discipline and who are content that Parliament should do very little, are able to look back on this period as a period of idyllic liberty. It is certain that such indiscipline was only possible in an aristocratic society and a society of small electorates where the selection and election of candidates could substantially be arranged by a few wealthy men meeting together in a private drawing-room. Essentially, as demands grew for further extension of the franchise and for measures of social reform, the groups concentrated into the two parties of the Victorian Parliamentary story—the Liberals and the Conservatives. Nationwide party organisations, hitherto unknown, were formed. Joseph Chamberlain, when still in his Radical days, formed a party organisation, based on American models, in Birmingham. Sir John Gorst copied him in the Conservative interest in 1874, and after Chamberlain had left the Liberal party the Newcastle Liberals attempted to fill the gap which he had left. Perhaps the formation of the new chamber which had been built after the destruction by fire of the old chamber of 1834 helped to bring this about. It so happened that the new chamber was built at the time when Gothic architecture was in fashion, and so the work was entrusted to two enthusiasts for the Gothic—Barry and Pugin—and the new chamber reproduced the rectangular form of St. Stephen's Chapel, as did the third chamber built after the Second World War. Had the old chamber been burnt a hundred years before, it would presumably have been rebuilt in classical style beneath a dome, and who can say what effect that might have had on the development of the party system? 'We shape our buildings,' said Churchill at the time of the building of the third chamber, and 'afterwards they shape us.'

The House of Commons in aristocratic days was a gentleman's club—the best club in Europe, as it was sometimes described. Its members had their party loyalties and played their party games. But their prime concern—far above the victory of their particular party— was that the system should work and that 'the Queen's Government should be carried on'. Therefore, aided by good sense and good will, they were able to carry on their business with a minimum of discipline and formal rules. Obstruction, it is true, was not quite unknown, but it was rare. Moriz, a Swiss Lutheran pastor, gives a vivid picture of the extraordinary informality of Parliamentary behaviour at the end of the eighteenth century. 'It is not at all uncommon,' he writes, 'to see a Member lying stretched out on one of the benches while others are debating; some crack nuts, others eat oranges or whatever else is in season. I have seen the Members bring their sons, while quite little boys, and carry them to their seats along with them.' In the course of time slightly stricter regulations were introduced. During the nineteenth century certain procedural changes were accepted. It was no longer allowed to interrupt the business of the House by debates on private petitions. The Government was able to increase the one day a week for government business to two days in 1837 and to three days in 1852. But there were still plenty of opportunities open to the private Member to interrupt debates; the House still remained predominantly a free house for private Members, and was only able to operate because they wished it to work and behaved themselves with restraint. Where necessary the Speaker was allowed to create new customs by his rulings.

Such good will was forthcoming from the Members from Great Britain. It could by no means be relied upon from the Members from Ireland. They had no feeling of loyalty to the British Parliamentary system. Far from wanting it to work, it was their ambition to prevent it from doing any other business so long as it refused to remedy the grievances of Ireland. In their view, they had been tricked into the Union by bribery and blackmail and had no mind to accept it. Thus most of the great Parliamentary issues of the nineteenth century were Irish issues. It was over Ireland that governments rose and fell. Catholic Emancipation was an Irish issue. The repeal of the Corn Laws was brought on by the Irish Famine. The time of Parliament in the years after that was very largely pre-occupied by the controversies of the Irish Church and the Irish land wars. We might almost say that the result of the Act of Union was that for a hundred years and more England was governed by Ireland, and when, towards the close of the century, Parnell succeeded to the Irish leadership he embarked on a regular campaign of obstruction the declared purpose of which was to make unworkable the life of Westminster, until a first priority was given to the remedy of Irish grievances. There had, it is true, been occasions before when Members resorted to obstruction, but it was Parnell who first imposed upon his followers a rigidity of discipline that had up till then been quite unknown at Westminster, and then used his authority to bring Parliamentary life to a standstill. He compelled his supporters to make use of their Parliamentary rights to talk endlessly on every subject that came up, whether of any real interest to them or not, and thus to prevent any business being done. Mr. Streathearn Gordon has calculated that in the 154 days of the session of 1885 fourteen Irish Members delivered 3,822 speeches, a daily average of

25 speeches. Matters came to a head over the Protection of Persons and Property (Ireland) Bill in 1881, when the Irish kept the House of Commons in session from four o'clock on Monday till half past nine on the Wednesday morning, when Mr. Speaker Brand, his papers, as was recorded, shaking in his hand, brought the session to a close by putting the question. To meet with Irish obstruction the House introduced various devices for curtailing its proceedings such as the closure, to prevent further speeches after a topic of debate had been exhausted. In 1887 W. H. Smith, then leader of the House, followed this up by the guillotine by which under certain circumstances the Speaker, or his deputy, can put amendments to the House to be voted without debate. These restrictions on debate, of course, still exist and in modern times, with the modern stress of legislation, are employed from time to time by every Government.

In 1902 Balfour by his so-called Railway Timetable effectively brought private Members still further under the control of the Executive. The Opposition always protest against the invocation of powers to limit debate, but their protests are somewhat synthetic as everyone knows that they employed them themselves in their day and will employ them again when they return to power.

The Irish interruption was an exception to the rule of honouring the conventions of behaviour on which the good order of the parliamentary system was based. But apart from that, the Victorian division of parties was of course between Liberals and Conservatives (and those whose memories stretch back to the years before the 1914 war remember a time when we grew up in the Gilbertian fashion, thinking that all mankind were naturally born to be either little Liberals or little Conservatives). With the passage of time the issues changed. Individuals sometimes crossed the floor of the House and transferred their allegiance from the one party to the other. But if a man left one party there was, as was generally thought, nowhere that he could go except to the other party. In the election of 1918 that followed on the Armistice, Lloyd

George's Government was returned with an enormous majority and the greater number of Members of the new Parliament were Conservatives. A return to the Conservative party was perhaps only to be expected and would not in itself have greatly mattered. But in the ordinary way the Liberals, even if defeated, would have been the second party and have formed the Opposition. As it was, the small Asquithian Liberal party was reduced to 46 Members and all its leaders without exception were defeated. At the next election in 1922 the Liberals fought as two separate groups, Asquithians and Lloyd Georgites, and did very badly. The Asquithians won 64 seats and the Lloyd Georgites 53. It was a Conservative victory. A year later at the next election in 1923 the two groups of Liberals had effected a fragile reunion and fought as an at any rate nominally united party. The Conservatives under Baldwin were defeated, but the most important issue at the election was whether the Liberals or Labour would succeed in returning as the stronger Opposition. It was a fairly close run race between them. Labour returned with 191 and the Liberals with 158. Had the Liberals just edged ahead of Labour, Asquith would presumably have been called on to form the Government. Whether he would have proved equal to the formation of an effective government, dependent as he would have been on the support of Labour votes and with the unity of his own party still fragile, is an open question. But it is at least possible that the Liberals would have succeeded in once more establishing themselves as the alternative party.

As it was, Asquith had no alternative but to put Ramsay Macdonald and the Labour party into office and the Liberals, caught in the middle between the two larger parties, have never since had the possibility of playing an effective part in Parliament. Compelled to choose between two division lobbies, a central party has little alternative but either irrevocably to attach itself as a mere wing to one of the main parties, as the National Liberals have done to the Conservatives, or else to split again and again as on issue after issue some go into one lobby and some into the other. This has been the fate of the Liberals who, over the years, have declined in number to the minuscule representation we know today. Experience in 1923 proved that the hope of a third smaller party to exert influence by holding the balance between the two major parties was doomed to failure. The public resented such claims and spectacularly punished the Liberals at the next election. They showed their demand that the candidates should be either of the Left or of the Right. It is true that in 1972 over the European Community issue the Liberals were able on a particular occasion to exercise a quite decisive influence, by their votes saving Mr. Heath's Government when its majority sank to eight, but they could not hope with such numbers to be in any way the permanent masters of the Government.

It is the fashion—particularly in some Labour circles—to assert that this decline of liberalism was inevitable, that the Liberals had had their day and that with the needs of the age it was inevitable that a Socialist party should take their place. It must be doubtful if this reasoning is true. Obviously the day for a nineteenth-century liberalism, devoted without qualification to capitalism and laissez-faire, had had its day and such a party could never have continued to carry the country. But was there any reason to think that the Liberal party would have remained the prisoner of such a creed? The whole record of the pre-1914 Liberal Government under Asquith and Lloyd George shows that it would not. That Government had shown itself enthusiastically ready to take the first steps towards the Welfare State and would certainly have been ready to advance further in that direction as opportunity offered. The issue between nationalisation and private enterprise was by no means as stark as it became the fashion to depict it. Winston Churchill at that date had been very ready to consider socialistic experiments. For instance in 1908 he called 'for a railways policy that would devise some form of state control'. A Liberal Government in the 1920s might well have shown itself ready to go as far in the direction of nationalisation as a lot of moderate Socialists wanted.

The failure of the Liberal party to reassert itself was not due to any insufficiency of Liberal ideas. The Liberals were often more fertile of ideas than the Members of either of the other parties. It was due to the fact that the architecture of our chamber and the habits of our minds clamour for two parties, the one party in Government and the other in Opposition, ready to fight against one another for the mastery of the State, but find it difficult to accommodate a third party which neither is nor has the hope of immediately becoming the Government. The electorate in Britain on election day nominally casts its votes for the individual candidates in its constituency. It was only with the 1970 election that the names of the parties have been admitted on to the ballot paper. A few electors do cast a personal vote, dictated by dislike or admiration for an individual candidate. The great majority vote the party ticket, vote because they wish the one party or the other to form the Government for the next five years. The individual voter will often avoid commitment to a party, thinking that there is something to be said for the one party and something for the other, but deciding that on balance one side rather than the other deserves his support. Mr. Ian Gilmour in his *The Body Politic* gives a reasoned defence of this attitude. It is, he argues, essential for good government that Parliament be predominantly divided into two parties, but there neither is nor should there be a clear-cut intellectual division between the parties. Both must in practice be essentially centralist; for a man who wishes to go into public life there is a balance of argument as between the two parties which he should choose, but, having made his choice, he must, save in the most exceptional circumstances, stand by it. There is a lot in this. Its weakness is that it compels the Member both in the House and on the platform to say a good deal that he does not fully believe. 'And what matter,' asks Mr. Gilmour, 'if the leaders do not always have complete belief in what they are saying?' This is more debatable. In the real world we have no doubt sometimes to equivocate with truth. But the man of integrity cannot feel comfortable if he is compelled to do so day after day. He may vote with his party. It is dangerous if he allows himself completely to think with it.

If we go back to the Middle Ages we find that in almost every country of Europe there were representative institutions of one sort or another. Then in the sixteenth and seventeenth centuries the absolute monarchs promised relief from the turbulence created by growing demands for popular power. In every country there was a conflict between the kings and the parliaments. But, whereas in England Parliament won that conflict, in the Continental countries victory went to the monarchs. Genuinely representative institutions withered. They only returned in the nineteenth century as the challengers to the claims of the absolute monarchs. Those nineteenth-century Parliaments were based on the admitted model of the British Parliament. They resembled the institutions of Britain except that they had a multitude of parties instead of the British two-party system.

3

Party Organisation

The obvious convenience of a two-party system is that it tends to give one party a clear majority. We avoid the instabilities of uneasy coalition from which other countries suffer. The price that we have to pay for this is that both parties must inevitably embrace a very considerable variety of opinions and are to a large extent coalitions themselves.

The formal organisation of the parliamentary parties at Westminster is as follows. When the Labour party is in opposition it has its Leader, its Deputy Leader, Chairman and Chief Whip, who are elected annually by vote of the Members. These four leaders, together with eight other Members elected by the Members of the House of Commons, and four peers elected by the Labour peers, form the Shadow Cabinet. The Leader of the party then allots the members of the Shadow Cabinet to supervise the various Government departments as he sees fit. He also appoints a number of other front-bench Opposition spokesmen.

When the party is in Government the Leader of the party is of course sent for by the Sovereign and appointed Prime Minister. In spite of certain demands that have at times been made, and in contrast to the custom in Australia, for instance, Labour Prime Ministers in Britain have firmly refused to allow the members of their Cabinet to be elected by the party and have kept in their own hands the freedom to form their ministry as they wished. The Prime Minister is not compelled to give appointments to members of the Shadow Cabinet. A liaison committee is set up to preserve contact between the Cabinet and its back-benchers. It consists of a chairman, a senior member of the party—probably an ex-minister—three vice-chairmen, a Labour peer, the Leader of the House of Commons and the Chief Whip. In addition there are frequent meetings between the Prime Minister and the Chairman of the party.

The organisation of the Conservative party is at any rate superficially different. All M.P.s of that party belong to the 1922 Committee, a committee formed in that year specifically to keep ministers in touch with back-bench opinion. Traditionally the leadership of the party emerged, as was said, out of some mysterious process of consultation and conversation behind the scenes. The back-bench Member was informed who had been selected and accepted the selection. When Sir Alec Douglas-Home was sent for to succeed Mr. Macmillan as Prime Minister there were protests that these mysterious processes were unsatisfactory and it was formally decided that in future the leader of the party should be selected by direct election by the Members of Parliament. It was by this process that Mr. Heath was elected Leader in 1965. The occasion has not yet occurred when either party has been called on to elect by ballot a Leader when it was itself in power.

When in opposition, the Conservative Leader, unlike the Leader of the Labour party, selects his own Shadow Cabinet. The back-benchers' right of election extends only to the election of the officers of the 1922 Committee. The Chairman of the 1922 Committee has a position of considerable influence with a right of direct access to the Prime Minister. When the party is in opposition, ex-ministers can always attend meetings of the 1922 Committee at will and just like any ordinary back-bencher. When the party is in government ministers can only attend by invitation.

When we were in Parliament, we who were Conservative made a certain habit of contrasting our freedom with the slavery under which the Labour Member lived. How great in practice is the contrast between the two parties is debatable. Professor Mackenzie in his *British Political Parties* tends to reach the conclusion that it is not very great. It is true that in theory the Leader of the Labour party is only elected for a year and the Conservative Leader's tenure is indefinite. But in practice the Conservatives seem to be more successful in getting rid of leaders when they no longer want them than is the Labour party. In spite of some criticism, Attlee was able to ride out all opposition and to remain Leader of the Labour party as long as he wished. Gaitskell was able to maintain his position in spite of all opposition until his death and would certainly have become Prime Minister had he survived until the Conservative defeat. At the moment of writing (1972) Mr. Wilson is still at the head of his party and there appears no immediate prospect of his deposition. On the other hand the Conservatives have changed their leadership from Winston Churchill to Anthony Eden, from Eden to Macmillan, from Macmillan to Douglas-Home and from Home to Heath. None of these, it is true, were deprived by any direct vote of no confidence from their followers, but with all of them resignation was preceded by a considerable volume of back-bench criticism. To what extent that criticism was responsible for their resignation is a matter of opinion. The Conservatives, it is certainly true, have much less belief in direct voting and formal election than have Labour. The members of the Shadow Cabinet are, as I say, not elected nor is the Chief Whip. The Leader has also direct control of the Central Office, where the Chairman of the party presides, and of the Research Department. All their officers are directly dependent on him.

In the Labour party the Leader has far less independent authority. Both the National Executive Committee and the Labour Party Conference at times have claimed the right to dictate policy to him. To what extent they have that right and to what extent they ought to have it is not quite clear. The National Executive Committee consists of twenty-eight members comprising the Leader and Deputy Leader and representatives from various organisations such as the Trade Unions, the constituency parties and the like. It is responsible to the Party Conference— that is to say, to the party outside Parliament. The party inside Parliament is the Parliamentary Labour Party. Documents can be quoted, and at the moment are being very vigorously quoted by, for instance, Mr. Wedgwood Benn, in favour of the thesis that the responsibility for settling Labour party policy rests with the Party Conference, but in practice Labour leaders, while naturally they would prefer to have the Party Conference on their side, are usually able to carry their own policy even if the Conference opposes it. Gaitskell's opposition to nuclear disarmament is a case in point. Similarly Mr. Wilson, in spite of resolutions pledging the country to abandon the independent nuclear deterrent, was able to defy such an obligation when he came into power. In practice a far greater difficulty for Labour Prime Ministers comes from left-wing dissidents within Parliament who insist on voting against party policy. There is on the other hand no question of Conservative leaders being in any way under the control of the Party Conference. Balfour said that he would as soon take dictation from his valet as from a Party Conference. The Conservative Party Conference is in fact more of a demonstration than a policy-making body. There are of course exceptions, such as when the Conference in 1954 voted to commit the party to building 300,000 houses—a commitment which Mr. Macmillan on becoming the Housing Minister was careful to fulfil, though it was well beyond what had previously been the ambition of the party platform.

Before Lloyd George became Prime Minister it was the custom for the Prime Minister, unless he was a peer, also to be the Leader of the House of Commons. When the Prime Minister was in the Lords, as with Rosebery and Salisbury, it was naturally necessary to appoint a special leader in the House of Commons. But this was thought of as a disadvantage and was accounted one of the reasons why it was no longer desirable that the Prime Minister should be in the Lords. Lloyd George, when he became Prime Minister, wishing to be free to devote all his time to the war, appointed Bonar Law to be the Leader of the Commons, and since the Second World War it has always been the custom of Prime Ministers to appoint a special Leader of the House. The term of office of those leaders is often short. The position in no kind of way implies for them any status as the second member of the Government or any right of succession. Still, it is a very important post. The Leader of the House has, of course, to answer to the Prime Minister for the way in which the Government's business is progressing and it is also his job so to conduct affairs that business is not more acrimonious than is inevitable, and that no Members or groups of Members are flagrantly denied their rights. Every Thursday he is cross-questioned for a few minutes at the end of question-time on the business of the coming week, and Members have the opportunity of raising any matter which they think of interest and which they think might usefully be debated in the House.

The officials who actually impose the party discipline

are the Whips. Whips, who were to begin with known as Whippers-in, an obvious reference to the hunting field, were not originally party officers. They date back to a time before there was a party system in the modern sense of the phrase. When the regular party organisations came to be formed it was common sense to appoint officers whose task would be to marshal their Members to vote the way in which the party wished them to vote. Today all parties or groups have their whips and every Member who wants to organise an agitation for any purpose will probably appoint some sympathiser to act as what may be called an *ad hoc* and temporary whip.

The everyday business of the House (the adjutant's work) is done by the Whips—the Chief Whip and his subordinates. It is his task to keep in touch with the Opposition Chief Whip and to arrange with him the details of the House's business. It is this liaison between the two Whips which is known as 'the usual channels'. It is obviously highly convenient both for them and for the House at large that these personal relations should be friendly and a great inconvenience when, as is alleged to be the case at the time of writing, the two Chief Whips are not on good terms with one another.

The Government Chief Whip holds the position of Parliamentary Secretary to the Treasury or Patronage Secretary. A number of the Assistant Whips hold various positions nominally in the Royal Household, and it is the duty of one of them every day to send a letter on the events in Parliament to the sovereign. The Opposition have a similar team of whips to the Government. The most important duty of the Government Whips is to prepare for the Leader of the House an essential timetable of business. It is their task to see that the Government gets its proposed business through in time, and they must keep an eye on the timetable and see that the Members of their party vote in the right division lobby when a division is called.

The word Whip has two separate meanings. It is used to describe the officers who perform these duties. It is also used to describe the document which is issued every week and distributed to all the Members of a party, telling them what will be the business of the House during the coming week and requiring their presence and support of the party in the division lobby. Whips are of three kinds: one-line, two-line and three-line, (i.e., underlines on the document). A one-line whip is of no especial moment and carries the implication that there will be no vote. A two-line whip implies a vote but not a vote of overwhelming importance: the Member's support in the lobby would be expected but not absolutely essential. If he can find a Member of the other party with whom he can pair, his absence would be excused. A three-line whip is very important. The Member is required to attend and vote. If it is absolutely impossible for him to do so, he must clear the matter beforehand with his Whip. If he fails to be present at the division, and has not arranged to be paired, he has to give an explanation to the Whips. In the last resort the Labour party reserves to itself the right to withdraw the whip from those who are persistently disobedient to party policy. This is tantamount to expulsion from the party and, if the whip were still withdrawn by the time that the next election came round, the rebel Member would not be selected as the party candidate. The weapon, however, is somewhat two-edged, for if the rebel Member chose to stand as an independent, he probably could not win against an official candidate but, by splitting the vote, would very likely let in a Conservative. A withdrawn whip is therefore nearly always restored before the election.

The Conservatives have never favoured the weapon of withdrawing the whip. There have from time to time been instances of Conservatives who have themselves resigned the whip in protest against party policy. The most notable in recent times was Harold Macmillan when he was in revolt against the policy of appeasement of the Chamberlain Government before the war. The effective weapon of discipline which the Whips possess is that of patronage. In fact they have a say in the nomination of all the minor jobs when a Government is formed. Winston Churchill in particular, by then a tired and ageing man, never bothered to get to know the younger Members of his party in the Parliament of 1945. As a result when he came to form the Government in 1951 few of the aspirants to minor office were known to him and their appointment was almost entirely left to be arranged by the Chief Whip. The Whips thus have opportunity for punishing, if punishment it be thought, Members who have consistently been un-disciplined. There is also a steady stream of appointments of one sort or another—parliamentary delegations abroad, delegates to the Council of Europe at Strasbourg—which fall to them and to which it is natural that they give first favour to those who have been most obedient.

As far as law or constitution goes, the Member's vote is absolutely free: the Whip has no authority over him. Whether or not a Member's revolt is in any way effective depends to a large extent on whether he has the support of his constituents. Aneurin Bevan for instance was able to defy his party whip in support of left-wing policies because he knew that his constituents at Ebbw Vale supported him in doing so. In general, Conservative members are tolerated by constituency associations when they deviate to the Right and Labour members when they deviate to the Left. Deviation towards a middle view is less popular, for those who serve on constituency associations are usually persons of very strong party loyalties. The uncommitted rarely bother with such activities. But in general, the rule of the Whips is accepted and even supported by Members. They perhaps grumble at the details of discipline. From time to time matters are left to a free vote and it is often said that the debates on such matters—as for instance on the abolition of capital punishment—are the House's best debates. There is a reality about them that is absent from the set debates. In the set debate, whoever gets the better of the exchange, it is certain how the vote will go at the end of it. In a free debate a Member is really speaking with the hope to make converts; the result is uncertain. And Members will often be found to suggest that there should be more free debates—that the party discipline is imposed on trivial details where it is quite unnecessary. In reply to that it is argued that the Government has to work to a programme and that if one motion, in itself trivial, is rejected, a whole timetable is upset. There is force in this argument, and Members in general are content to see themselves as returned to Parliament either to sustain or to oppose the Government. The vast multiplicity of matters on which a Member has to record his opinion in a division lobby is such that it would be quite impossible for him to have a real opinion on all of them. He is grateful for a machinery which makes up his mind for him.

When I went into Parliament in 1945 the Conservative Chief Whip was James Stuart. He was afterwards succeeded by Patrick Buchan Hepburn (now Lord Hailes). Both were reasonably popular and accepted. Serious revolt against the party was rare but there was among the back-benchers a good deal of light-hearted banter against the Whips, of the type that might be found against a reasonably popular school prefect. How much they enjoyed this and how much they resented it, it is difficult to say. Secluded in their own room, they lead a life somewhat removed from that of the rest of us in the smoking-room or the bar. One of the most important qualities required by a whip is a sense of humour and a capacity not to take too seriously what does not deserve excessive consideration. Under Buchan Hepburn one of the junior whips was Edward Heath. It is the custom that whips never speak in a debate. This is because it is so important that they should preserve as good personal relations as possible and therefore it is thought important that they should not entangle themselves in exchanges either with opponents or with colleagues. It therefore resulted that we other Members never had an opportunity of learning Edward Heath's talents as a debater. He was mainly known for his curious habit of shaking his shoulders like a jelly when he laughed. We hardly guessed his real abilities. His career has in fact proved quite unique. Chief Whips are generally chosen for administrative ability but not thought of as men of great creative power. They go from their post to positions of dignity but not of quite the first rank. James Stuart became Secretary for Scotland, Buchan Hepburn Governor-General of the ill-starred Federation of the West Indies. Edward Heath, of humbler social origins than they, is the only man ever to have risen from Chief Whip to become Prime Minister.

The Labour party believes more in formal organisation and in voting than do the Conservatives. They vote at their party committees, which the Conservatives almost never do. They elect by secret ballot their Shadow Cabinet and their Chief Whip. They have a formal constitution to which their candidates have to pledge obedience. Before being adopted the Labour candidate has, according to the code of conduct of the Parliamentary Labour Party, to agree that no reservations of private judgement 'entitle members to vote contrary to a decision of a party meeting, or to abstain from voting on a vote of confidence in a Labour Government'. In 1945 when the Labour party had an immense majority they felt free to relax their rules and a number of left-wingers fairly consistently voted against Ernest Bevin's foreign policy. When 1950 greatly narrowed their majority they had to reimpose a strict discipline and rebellious votes were no longer tolerated. The Conservative candidate is not required to take any formal pledge. But in practice rebellious votes are somewhat more common on the Labour benches than on the Conservative. The Conservative party is a pragmatic party, concerned to get things done and to see that the country is governed. The only Conservative principle is that it is for the public interest that a Conservative Government should be in power. To weaken the party by overt divisions weakens its power to achieve this purpose. The purposes of a good number of Labour members are of much the same pragmatic kind, but there are always on the Labour benches a number of more dogmatic Socialists, more concerned with keeping unsullied their devotion to an ideal vision than with day-to-day achievements. As a result, every leader of the Socialist party, Ramsay Macdonald, Attlee, Gaitskell, Wilson, has had fairly frequently to deal with left-wing revolts against his policy, revolts which were carried as far as the division lobby. Ernest Bevin's foreign policy of opposition to Communism and friendship with America was widely attacked by his own back-benchers. In practice, whatever the theoretical differences, Professor Mackenzie is probably right in saying that the differences between the ways in which the two parties organise their lives are not as great as it is sometimes the fashion to pretend. Besides, the overt clashes between the parties on the floor of the House are by no means the whole of Parliamentary business. If the country and Parliament are to go on at all there is a vast mass of business that has to be done much the same whichever party is in power. As Churchill once put it, 'four fifths of one party always agrees with four fifths of what the other party are doing'.

There are numerous all-party activities. There is also the all-important social life that takes place in the smoking-room or the bar. Members vary very much from one another in their attitude towards such activities. Some keep themselves very much to themselves and mix little with those who are not of their own party. Others—and among them some who are most vigorous and controversial in debate—are very easy mixers outside the chamber, and it will be common enough to see two Members who have been lambasting one another with acrimony in the chamber go off afterwards to the bar for a glass of beer. No one was more generous and catholic in his personal friendship than Aneurin Bevan. In the immediately post-war Parliament Sir Waldron Smithers won for himself among Socialists a reputation as a figure of quite comical reaction, but there was nobody for whom those Socialist Members had a greater personal affection. It is in the smoking-room or the bar that a Member learns about those of a different background and opinion from himself in a way that the keen politician who is not in Parliament may never have the opportunity to do, and many would think that this broader education which Membership gives is among its most important advantages.

The organisation of the House of Lords is similar to, though much less rigid than that of the Commons. Party discipline is much looser. There, too, each of the parties has its Leader and its Whip. The only difference is, of course, that the Conservative have always a large majority. This means that they can always carry a motion when the Conservatives are in power and defeat one when Labour is in power. But, quite apart from the precise restrictions of the Parliament Acts, the peers have to vote under the knowledge that their amendments will have to go back to the Commons and, if directly hostile to the Commons' will, are likely to be reversed there. The Lords will have in the end to give way. Therefore wise Conservative leadership, as for instance that of Lord Salisbury after 1945, is careful not to take rough advantage of its majority in the Upper House and not to give a direct rejection to measures that the Commons has clearly approved. They debate in the consciousness that persistence in obstruction would merely lead to their own suppression.

4

The Prime Minister and the Cabinet

It is the Sovereign who commissions some statesman to form a Government, but the Prime Minister, once commissioned, has the right to choose his own colleagues. The appointments have, of course, to receive the formal approval of the Sovereign. Today it is hardly possible that the Queen would formally refuse to accept any appointment suggested to her, though it is possible that out of private tact a Prime Minister might refrain from suggesting the name of some statesman whom he knew to be highly obnoxious to her. The Prime Minister appoints all the other ministers and he can at any time demand the resignation either of an individual minister or of the whole Cabinet. It is also his right to ask the Sovereign for a dissolution of Parliament. He is therefore in a very strong position and throughout this century the dominance of the Prime Minister over the Cabinet has steadily increased. Balfour at the beginning of the century had little control over his ministers. Joseph Chamberlain was both a more forceful and a more powerful man than he. His ministers dropped off from him, some to Free Trade, and some to Protection, over the tariff-reform controversy. Campbell Bannerman proved himself able to reunite his apparently divided party but he did not live long enough to show whether he would have been a dominant Prime Minister. Asquith after him presided over what is very often spoken of as the ablest Cabinet that has ever ruled over this country. Among such ministers he could not hope to be more than *primus inter pares*. But Lloyd George, who had the advantage (or disadvantage) that he was not supported by a regular party, was able to establish a much more personal rule until eventually his Conservative supporters turned against him and dismissed him. Bonar Law's premiership was only a short interlude. After him Baldwin was at first little-known and, when he plunged his party into an election about Protection in which he was defeated, seemed to have destroyed his career; but a year afterwards he came back to power and ruled the country for five years until 1929. Then in 1931 he returned as a member of the National Government and on Ramsay Macdonald's retirement succeeded him as Prime Minister. In the years between 1924 and 1929 he was challenged by the formidable personality of Winston Churchill as Chancellor of the Exchequer but he so succeeded in imposing himself that he was able to dispense with Churchill's support in his third Government. Neville Chamberlain was his leading subordinate in that Government but it was notable that, though they held radically differing views on foreign policy, Neville Chamberlain, so long as he was merely Chancellor of the Exchequer, was quite unable to give any expression to his views. It was only when he became Prime Minister that he could attempt to implement them.

During the war Churchill was certainly master in his own house, though the circumstances were so exceptional as to make it impossible to draw general lessons from that experience. After the war Attlee ruled by holding the balance between his competing subordinates. Churchill in his second term of office was an old and stricken man and unable to play again the dominant part he had played during the war. Eden when he became Prime Minister was an ill man and according to all accounts did not so much dominate his ministers as niggle them by continual worrying interference. Yet whether or not the action was wise, he was able at the time of Suez to carry the country into war without apparently consulting the members of his Cabinet. Macmillan, when he succeeded him, had the very difficult task of wholly reversing the Suez policy and of winning the nation's consent to that reversal. He did this and did it with such success that he was able to snatch victory out of what appeared to be certain defeat. When he was forced by ill health to retire, the party was left with a difficult task in finding a successor. Sir Alec Douglas-Home was never able fully to make himself master of his Government. His two successors, Mr. Wilson and Mr. Heath, are too near to us for final judgement on their achievements but whatever else may be said about them, at least it cannot be pretended that they have kept their followers in any doubt that a determined Prime Minister is very effectively the leader of his party and government.

How much those who served under modern Premiers like them is hard to say. For the public the sudden news of a resignation is the first that we have usually heard of what we afterwards learn were long smouldering difficulties. The Premier today turns on his colleagues when things are going ill, and, as with Macmillan, deals out to them wholesale dismissals. Victorian Prime Ministers never dismissed their colleagues for inefficiency. The colleagues resigned, when they did resign, on a difference of opinion. The general truth seems to be that Prime Ministers are not much liked by their colleagues and perhaps it is just as well that they should not be. It is idle to complain that they are not always very likeable men. The battle for the summit is a bitter battle and likeable men may not reach the top. Yet Prime Ministers are not there to be merely popular. As Gladstone in his old age said to his young Home Secretary Asquith, 'If you ever have to form a Cabinet, Asquith, play the butcher.' Perhaps Asquith did not play it sufficiently.

The members of the cabinet are Privy Councillors, forbidden by oath to reveal its secrets. Its meetings are private meetings. It was not until the First World War that there was in modern times any secretarial record of its decisions other than the private daily letter which the Prime Minister or a whip wrote to the Sovereign and of which no one else saw a copy. For our knowledge of how the Cabinet works, we have recently had Tom Jones's accounts of the workings of the Cabinet that negotiated the Irish Treaty, and Mr. Wilson has written more fully than had previously been the custom about the workings of his own Cabinet. But in general we are dependent on indiscreet reminiscences of members of past Cabinets or the general accounts of those who have sat in Cabinets, such as those left by Herbert Morrison in *Government and Parliament*. The Cabinet generally, though not quite always, meets in the Cabinet Room at the Prime Minister's house at 10, Downing Street. Those who are members of the Cabinet attend its meeting by right. Other ministers and sometimes other officials—civil servants or members of the Chiefs of Staff—may be summoned to it if matters on which they can give expert evidence are to be discussed. Even if we had the full knowledge it would be difficult to give a succinct account of how Cabinet meetings are conducted for, according to the description of those who have sat in a Cabinet, Prime Ministers differ widely from one another in their manner of presiding. The Cabinet room is a longish room decorated in white with touches of gold. At one end French windows open on to the garden of No. 10, at the other double doors open on to the Prime Minister's private secretarial offices. On the side opposite the fireplace are large windows opening on to the Horse Guards Parade and the Admiralty. The entrance is by double doors from the hall. When he is ready the Prime Minister himself or a secretary appears and summons the ministers to enter. They take their seats round the table covered with green baize. The Prime Minister sits with his back to the fireplace. An agenda has been placed at each seat and under the Prime Minister's presidency the discussion proceeds. Cabinet papers have been circulated by anyone who wishes to bring up some particular matter. Votes are rarely taken. The more normal plan is, after a sufficiency of opinions have been expressed, for the Prime Minister to sum up, as he sees it, the general sense of the Cabinet. After the meeting is finished it is the duty of the secretaries, who have been busy taking notes, to circulate the summary of the conclusions that have been reached. The discovery of the solution to complicated and technical problems is in modern times often remitted to special Cabinet committees—not to be confused with party committees, committees of the Whole House or standing committees to deal with bills in progress. Of these Cabinet committees not very much is known. Neither their personnel nor their tasks are generally published.

Whether acting under the dictatorship of the Prime Minister or not, the Cabinet is usually able to carry its policies through Parliament. In the years since the First World War there have been only three occasions when the Cabinet's policies have been rejected by the House of Commons. The first was in 1924 when the House voted against the Government's refusal to prosecute the Scottish Communist, Mr. Campbell. In that Parliament, however, the Government was only a minority Government, the votes of the Liberals and Conservatives combined exceeding that of the Government's Labour supporters. The second was in 1931 when the Labour Government fell and the National Government took its place. The third was in 1940 when Chamberlain's Government, though not actually defeated, was deserted by a sufficient number of his supporters to make it impossible for him to carry on.

5

The Officers of Parliament

By far the most important officer in the House of Commons is the Speaker. Sergeant Yelverton in Queen Elizabeth's reign laid down the qualities that are required of him. 'A man, big comely, stately and well spoken, his voice great, his carriage majestical.' The line of Speakers stretches back unbroken to Sir Thomas Hungerford in 1377. In medieval times the Speaker was looked on as the King's representative in Parliament. He derived his title from the fact that it was his duty to give expression to the Sovereign of the Commons' wishes. In doing so he was indeed supposed to pay attention both to the wishes of the Commons and to those of the Sovereign. But between the two it was the Sovereign to whom he primarily owed obedience. It was said for instance by Sir Edward Coke, who was Speaker from 1593 to 1598, that 'having mastered the difficult art of serving two masters, he showed a remarkable dexterity . . . in order to comply with the wishes of the Queen.' (Philip Laundy, *The Office of Speaker*, p. 182). The Commons had a theoretical voice in the election of their Speaker but their selection was subject to royal approval. Their voice was likened by Sir Edward Coke to the *congé d'élire* for a bishop by which the Dean and Chapter are given the right to validate the election of a prelate whom the Sovereign has already in fact appointed. Doubtless Charles I, miscalculating, thought that he could rely on Speaker Lenthall's support when he forced his way into the Commons to arrest the five Members. Lenthall to Charles's surprise showed that he interpreted his duty as owing obedience to the House rather than to the monarch. He said that he had 'neither eyes to see nor tongue to speak but as the House is pleased to direct'.

A result of the Civil War was that the Speaker was recognised as henceforth owing his primary loyalty to the House. It is true that after it has selected its Speaker the House has still to submit his name to the Sovereign and he is not Speaker until his election has received the royal approval. In 1679 Charles II refused that approval, but such a thing has never happened again and is as unlikely to happen again as is the refusal of the royal assent to a bill that has been passed through Parliament. After the Restoration, when the Speaker was at all under suspicion, it was not because he was thought to be the creature of the Sovereign so much as because he was thought to be too much the creature of the party in power. Harley, for instance, in 1705 combined the Speakership with the position of Secretary of State. Lloyd George when he was Prime Minister issued a crudely blunt press announcement from Downing Street: 'The Prime Minister has offered the Speakership to Mr. Whitley.' In modern times Members on the back benches are always suspicious of any attempt by a consortium of the front benches to plant on them a Speaker. When Mr. Speaker Lloyd was proposed in 1970, there was grumbling on the back benches not against him personally but at the suggestion that he had been foisted on them by a conspiracy of the two front benches. It was also complained, when Speaker Lloyd was elected, that it was undesirable to have in the Chair one who had held high and controversial ministerial office. Shakespeare Morrison had indeed also held ministerial office, though not of so high or controversial a nature as Mr. Lloyd's, but in general the post is offered to those who have not held office.

The health and prestige of the House depends more on the Speaker than on any other Member. A weak and incompetent Speaker, or one who showed himself manifestly partisan, could very rapidly deal to the standing of the House an irreparable damage. Yet the traditions by which the Speaker keeps himself utterly divorced from any activities that are in any way controversial is comparatively recent. Even when Speakers after Harley ceased to be ministers there was very little pretence at impartiality prior to the rule of Speaker Onslow from 1728 to 1761. In modern times a Speaker, having once been Speaker, never returns again to ordinary back-bench membership. On retirement he always accepts a peerage. But Addington in 1802 left the chair to become Prime Minister. Shaw Lefevre who sat from 1839 to 1857 is generally regarded as the first of the modern Speakers who imposed on himself a rigid divorce from all private interests.

In 1945, when I arrived at Westminster, the Labour party had just come to office with their triumphant majority. They were in a mood of high confidence and, as will be remembered, signalised the first meeting of the new House by singing the Red Flag. The Labour Party had never had a Labour Speaker and it would have been intelligible if in their demand for a universal brave new world they had insisted among other changes on a Labour Speaker. It is the general custom that, though on a vacancy the party in power has the right to nominate the new Speaker, once a Speaker is in the Chair he is continued in office in the new Parliament even if the balance of parties has changed. Speaker Clifton Brown, a Conservative, was in the Chair at the time of the 1945 election and with great restraint the new Labour ministers decided to honour the old tradition and keep him there rather than elect a Labour Speaker. Speaker Clifton Brown had expected to be dismissed and was much moved—reduced to tears, it is said—by the amazing generosity of Attlee and William Whitely the Labour Chief Whip, in deciding to keep him in office. Speaker Clifton Brown was not a very distinguished or brilliant man but performed very honourably and competently the task which chance imposed upon him of guiding the first steps of the new sort of House of Commons with its Labour majority. The transition was more smoothly made under his direction than it would have been with a Labour Speaker whose election would probably have been contested. Clifton Brown remained in the Chair until 1951. The election of that year gave the Conservatives a majority. There were some on the Labour benches who thought that the party's abnegation six years before ought to be rewarded by the Conservatives allowing the election of a Labour Speaker. Major Milner, a Labour Member from Leeds, had been Chairman of Ways and Means, or Deputy Speaker, under the previous Speaker and was, it was argued, well qualified for the post. However the Conservatives elected to stand on their rights as a majority and put up Shakespeare Morrison as their candidate. A contested election was held which ran on straight party lines and therefore gave the Conservative Morrison victory over the Labour Milner. Fortunately it was possible to fight it out without great acrimony and Morrison received the loyal support of all Members of both parties after his election. He was a witty and companionable man and made an excellent Speaker. When he resigned in 1959 the Conservatives were still in the majority in the House of Commons and there was no challenge to the election of a Conservative, Hylton-Foster, to succeed him. By the time that Hylton-Foster died in 1965 Labour was in office. There therefore could now be no challenge of their right at last to select a Labour Speaker. It was the last citadel of power which Labour had never as yet captured and therefore it was a matter of considerable importance that a worthy candidate should be found to occupy it. Fortunately such a candidate was forthcoming and Dr. Horace King proved himself by general consent one of the outstanding Speakers and in every way worthy of his great predecessors. When Dr. King had to resign in 1970 the Conservatives were in power and they nominated Selwyn Lloyd to succeed him. There were protests against Selwyn Lloyd, as we have said, from back-benchers who alleged that he had been foisted on them by a conspiracy of the front benches. However he was elected, but the times have proved to be turbulent at Westminster, and he has by no means always had an easy passage.

Etiquette demands of the Speaker that he seclude himself from the general social life of the House. He does not go into the smoking-room, the Library—still less into any of the bars. He does not eat in the Members' dining-room. He lives apart in his own lodgings. On parade he wears court dress and on state occasions a gold embroidered gown over it. He has his own Speaker's Coach which is drawn by two drayhorses from Whitbread's brewery for State occasions. In the House he wears a black silk gown over his court dress and also a full-bottomed wig. Each day before the meeting of the House, he walks in procession through the central lobby, preceded by his chaplain and the mace which has to be laid on the table before the House is properly in session.

When an election for a new Speaker is to be held, the Clerk of the House presides. From his seat at the table he points with a finger at the Member who has been selected to propose the candidate. The mace is then under the table. The Member makes his proposition. It is seconded and, if desired, opposed. When the Speaker has been elected the proposers have to pretend to drag him to the chair and the elected candidate has to make a show of forcible resistance. This of course is a relic of the days when, owing to royal displeasure, the Speakership carried with it a certain risk. Now the election is not formally completed until the royal assent has been received. Only then is the mace placed on the table and the House formally in session.

The Speaker is a Member of Parliament. When an election comes he has to stand for election just like any other Member. But he stands as Speaker and not as a member of any party. For this reason he is often allowed to be unopposed and, when opposed, is usually opposed by an independent candidate with some grievance rather than by a regular party member. In his campaign he must not enter into any of the dominant controversies of the day and his constituents have sometimes been heard to complain that they are thus in a measure disfranchised. On the other hand he can fairly answer, as Speaker Clifton

Brown once explained to me, that he has many private opportunities to call attention to private grievances greatly superior to those of the ordinary Member; and, though the suggestion has sometimes been made that a fictitious constituency of St. Stephens should be created for which the Speaker should nominally sit, no great interest has ever been taken in the proposal.

It is the duty of the Speaker during a debate when a Member who has been speaking resumes his seat and other Members who wish to take part in the debate rise in their place, to select and call the name of one who is said to 'catch the Speaker's eye'. It is important of course that he should preserve a reputation for impartiality in his selections, and it is the general habit of the Speaker to call Members alternately from the one side and the other. It is a custom that a Privy Councillor can generally expect to be called whenever he rises in his place. This privilege of the Privy Councillor is greatly resented by back-bench Members who are not Privy Councillors. No one who has not experienced it can understand the nervous frustration of a day spent fruitlessly 'bumping' as it is called—that is to say, rising in one's place time and again only to hear another Member called in one's stead.

The Speaker does not himself intervene in the debate and, though there is no law or Standing Order to forbid it, he does not in fact use his vote when a division is called. The only occasion when he votes is when there is a tie and then he votes not in accordance with his own opinion on the matter discussed but in such a way as to maintain the status quo, or, if possible, to enable the matter to be discussed again.

The Speaker has all the duties of keeping order which pertain to any chairman of any meeting at any place. If the words of the Member who is addressing the House are irrelevant to the subject under debate or if he is guilty of tedious repetition the Speaker must call him to order. It is the Speaker's duty to call to order, and to demand a retraction from any Member who uses unparliamentary expressions about another Member. If a Member defies the

Chair and refuses to accept his ruling the Speaker can order him to leave the chamber. If he persists in defiance he can 'name' him. When he does this a motion is at once moved, probably by the Leader of the House, suspending the defiant Member from the service of the House. If there is gross and continuous disorder the Speaker can suspend the sitting of the House for a certain period and this in the present troublous times Mr. Speaker Lloyd has had to do on a number of occasions. I do not recollect any occasion when the sitting was suspended in the years immediately after the war, which were more tranquil. Rules of Order are since Parnell much stricter today than they were in the nineteenth century.

The Speaker is the servant of the House but, as long as he is in the Chair, his rulings must be obeyed. If a Member or Members are dissatisfied they must not immediately defy him, but they always have the right to put down a substantive motion to censure him. Were such a motion to be carried the Speaker would presumably have to resign, but no question of that happening has ever arisen in modern times. From time to time motions have been put down but they have almost always been to call attention to some particular point and have rarely been pressed to a division. The House did divide on a motion on the Deputy Speaker, Sir Robert Grant Ferris, in February 1972, but the motion was defeated. The only Speaker to be deposed by a vote of the House was Trevor in 1695 who was involved in corruption over army contracts. In the conduct of the debate it is the business of the House, which means in fact of the Government, to decide when the closure should be invoked; if the Chief Whip moves the closure it rests with the Speaker to decide whether he will accept the motion. It also rests with him to decide whether he will accept a motion for the adjournment of the House to consider a specific and important matter. Until recently the restrictions on these debates were so tight that it was hardly ever possible to get the Speaker's leave, but in 1967 the powers of the Speaker to grant them were greatly widened. He also has the very important power of deciding, when faced with amendments to a motion, whether an amendment shall or shall not be called. His general rule is to accept amendments that he thinks of substance but not to allow the House to waste its time on the discussion of those which are essentially repetitive of what has been already discussed.

The importance of the task of the Speaker and the necessity to keep the House in as good a humour as possible is therefore very clear. He has three principal assistants: the Chairman of Ways and Means and the two Deputy Chairmen. These officers are of less importance than the Speaker. They preside over the House, sitting at the Clerks' table when the House is in Committee (see p. 104) and, seated in the Chair, over the full House when the Speaker is absent, but they do not wear the Speaker's robes. They have the normal powers of discipline, but they cannot adjourn the House in case of disturbance. If such action should be called for they have to summon the Speaker.

The presiding officer of the House of Lords is the Lord Chancellor, but his role is very different from that of the Speaker. He is usually, and has always been in modern times, a peer, but no law compels him to be one and the Lord Chancellor still presides over the Lords even if he is a Commoner. Sir Thomas More is an obvious case in point. Unlike the Speaker, the Lord Chancellor is a member of the Cabinet and, though he does not usually take a very prominent part in party quarrels, still there is no pretence that he is without opinions. He can take part in debate and express his own views; when he does so, he steps a foot or two away from the Woolsack. Apart from being a member of the cabinet and the Speaker of the House of Lords, he is also head of the judiciary and sits as a law lord when the House of Lords has to hear appeals.

His authority as Speaker of the House is very limited. He puts the question and, unlike the Speaker in the Commons, votes in debates, but he has no casting vote. In the event of a tie in the Lords the motion is not carried. The House of Lords has never been submitted to any Parnellite system of obstruction and has therefore never had to draft for itself strict rules of procedure. The Lord Chancellor has no power to call a noble lord to order. The speaker can in general stray as widely as he wishes. If his remarks should become too intolerable it is for another peer to move that 'the noble lord be no longer heard', and for the other peers to vote him down. The Lord Chancellor does not select and call those who are to speak in a debate. The proposed speakers are arranged and published in a list before the debate begins. If through any confusion two lords should rise at the same time, the House itself decides by shouting which of them it wishes to hear. Speakers do not, as in the Commons, address the Chair. They address the House, speaking to it collectively as 'My Lords'. The Lord Chancellor is a political officer and works in collaboration with the Leader of the House and the Chief Whip. When he is absent the Chair is taken by one of his deputies of whom the chief is the Lord Chairman of Committees. The House of Lords, like the Commons is a rectangular building, with red benches, gilded furnishings and stained-glass windows. At its far end is the royal throne, in front of the Throne, the Woolsack. The front bench immediately to the right of the Lord Chancellor is for the bishops. Otherwise peers range themselves on the two sides of him as supporters of the Government or Opposition, as in the Commons. There are also there, as there are not in the Commons, cross benches for those who do not wish to align themselves with any party. For a division Members cry out not as in the Commons, 'Aye' or 'No' but 'Content' or 'Not Content'.

Both Houses have also their officials to serve them. In the House of Commons the first of these officials are the Clerks, three of whom sit side by side at the Speaker's feet as he presides in the Chair. When the House goes into Committee (see p. 104) the Chairman or Deputy Chairman of Ways and Means takes one of the seats at this table. The chief of these clerks is known as the Clerk of the House. His is a post of great antiquity dating back to

Robert de Melton in 1363. He is appointed for life by the Crown on the advice of the Prime Minister. Beneath him is a Clerk's department which is staffed by members who have passed the Civil Service examination. It is the duty of the Clerk to advise both the Speaker and other Members of Parliament on the practice of the House. It is today, for instance, a matter of considerable intricacy what are and what are not admissible as subjects for questions to ministers. Members hand in their questions and may then soon afterwards receive a request from the Clerk to call at the table to discuss the question. A short conversation with one of the Clerks takes place, the Member perched at his side while the debate goes on around them. The Clerk points out that for such and such a reason this is a question that cannot properly appear on the Order Paper. In all probability the Member bows to the Clerk's experience and takes his advice, but the Clerk has of course no authority over Members. He is merely an adviser. The only authority which can rule a question definitely out of order is the Speaker, and if the Member challenges the Clerk's ruling he is always at liberty to carry the matter up to the Speaker. But most frequently the Clerk's interpretation is accepted as sufficient. The Clerk of the House has under him a department of, at present, forty clerks distributed among the main branches of the House's business. It is the duty of these always to give assistance and advice to Members and of course in modern times it is a very strict obligation on them to give their advice with complete impartiality. They will be as ready to advise how a proposition can be presented as they will be to advise how it can be rebutted. It has not always been so. In the seventeenth and the eighteenth centuries the clerks were paid directly by the Treasury and interpreted it as their duty to see the Treasury business through the House. They also received private fees from those involved in the passage of legislation, whether Members of Parliament or others. It was only in 1800 that an Act of Parliament established regular Commissioners for House of Commons Offices, of whom the Speaker and the Chancellor of the Exchequer were two, forbade private fees and established for the clerks a regular system of official salaries. The system was again reviewed later in the century by Speakers Shaw Lefevre and Denison between 1839 and 1872 and survives essentially in the same form to this day.

The Clerk of the House is also the accounting officer for the House of Commons vote. It is one of his duties to account to the Public Accounts Committee for the House's expenditure. This gives him a measure of control over the Serjeant-at-Arms and the other departments of the House. The Serjeant-at-Arms is the officer who carries the mace in the Speaker's procession which precedes each sitting of the House. He sits at the end of the chamber opposite the Speaker's Chair and is responsible for order in the chamber. If a recalcitrant Member has to be expelled from the chamber it is he who is called upon to carry out the Speaker's orders. The police and porters who keep order in the galleries are in his control. Another department runs the Library, and provides research services for Members.

The Lords provide similar services to those of the Commons. The Clerk of the House of Lords there is called the Clerk of the Parliaments. The official title of the Clerk of the Commons is the Under Clerk of the Parliaments. The Clerk of the Parliaments appoints the other clerks subordinate to him, similar in nature though fewer in number to those in the Commons. Some of them are detailed to the judicial work.

II

THE MEMBERSHIP OF PARLIAMENT

1

The House of Lords

In spite of the dominance of the Commons, Parliament is not a single-chamber legislature. The size of the House of Lords has varied greatly over the years. If we go back to the Middle Ages, to begin with, the two Houses did not sit separately. They assembled together in the presence of the King to form a Parliament. The separate meetings of the Commons and the Lords which took place subsequently were unofficial committee meetings. The privilege of the Commons to initiate financial legislation, granted to them by Henry IV, gave the Commons reason for their separate meetings. But it was not until Henry VIII's time that a special House of Lords was regularly established. The peers of the realm killed one another off in the Wars of the Roses and by Henry VII's accession there were only thirty-two secular peers. They were greatly outnumbered by the spiritual peers who at that time included not only the bishops but also the mitred abbots and indeed four Lady Abbesses, from Wilton, Shaftesbury, Barking and Winchester.

The Tudor monarchs created a number of new peers and during the first half of the seventeenth century before the Civil War the number fluctuated between 70 and 150. After the Restoration the number markedly increased and the unions with Scotland and Ireland brought further increases. At the Treaty of Utrecht peers were specially created to make a majority for the Treaty. Afterwards the suggestion was made that the royal prerogative to create further new peers should be limited to five, but the proposal was defeated. Yet there were not a large number of new creations during the earlier eighteenth century. It was the younger Pitt who recklessly increased the number at the end of the century. Since then there have been steady further creations until in 1968 there were 736 hereditary peers, 122 peers of first creation, 155 life peers, 23 law lords and 26 bishops—making a total of 1,062. The number has steadily increased since, but is still of that order. In the Middle Ages it was by no means clearly defined who was and who was not a peer, and the monarchs were able to keep in their own hands considerable freedom of choice as to who they would summon to Parliament. It was not finally settled that a peer had an absolute right to a summons, whether or not the King liked it, until Charles I attempted to refuse a summons to his political opponent, the Earl of Bristol, in 1625. It was then decided that the King had no right to 'refuse a writ to a peer capable of sitting in Parliament'.

The Reform Act of 1832 was not only of importance in the history of the House of Commons. The Houses had already in the 1820s clashed over Catholic Emancipation, the Commons being for it and the Lords against. The conflict came to a head over the Reform Act and out of that conflict arose the tacit settlement on which the relations between the two Houses were based for the next eighty years. The Lords accepted that the Commons were the masters of taxation. The Commons accepted that the Lords had a veto on legislation. The Duke of Wellington pronounced that the Lords might use their veto to delay legislation on which it thought that the Commons were misrepresenting public opinion. It might compel the Commons to test public opinion by a new election, but if the Commons were really determined on a measure, as they were for Reform, and if there was no reason to think that they did not have public opinion behind them, then the Lords had no alternative but to accept the Commons' verdict. As Lord Lyndhurst put it in 1858, 'It is also a most important part of our duty to check the inconsiderate rash, hasty and undigested legislation of the other House, but not to make a firm determined and persevering stand against the opinion of the other House when that opinion is backed by the opinion of the people.' This did not mean that the Lords had to reduce themselves to a mere stamp and on at least one occasion in the nineteenth century they were able to play a notable part, entirely in obedience to this interpretation of their function: that was when they rejected Gladstone's Second Home Rule Bill. Whether that bill was good or bad, it was certainly unpopular, as the subsequent general election showed, and the Lords were entirely justified in throwing it out.

Palmerston attempted to reform the Lords by introducing life peerages, but the attempt was defeated. The Lords in their constitution remained unreformed. Nevertheless throughout all the nineteenth century a Liberal could not fail to reflect that, though the Lords might in general behave with moderation, and though the great majority of peers might never attend the House, yet the majority of peers were impenitently Conservative and there was always a danger that the back-woods peers might be called up to vote down any Liberal measure. 'When the Conservative party is in power,' wrote Lord Rosebery to Queen Victoria in April, 1894, 'there is practically no House of Lords; it takes whatever the Conservative Government brings it from the House of Commons without question or dispute; but the moment a Liberal Government is formed, this harmless body assumes an active life, and its activity is entirely exercised in opposition to the Government.' 'Nearly, if not quite, half the Cabinet is in favour of a single chamber,' he wrote a little later. 'The more prominent people of the Liberal party appear to be of the same opinion.'

From the time of the ruling on the Earl of Bristol until modern days not only had a peer the absolute right to be summoned to Parliament but it was impossible for him to get out of being a peer even if he wanted to. An act of 1876 created life law lords but, with their exception, the constitution of the House of Lords remained unchanged until modern times. When the first Lord Hailsham died his son,

Quintin Hogg, tried to get out of inheriting the peerage, wishing to remain in the Commons, but Attlee, who was then Prime Minister, would do nothing to help him. When Lord Stansgate died, Mr. Anthony Wedgwood Benn had better fortune. He stood again at the bye-election for his constituency in Bristol and, though he could not then take his seat, succeeded in getting himself elected. His defeated opponent was allowed to take the seat. The absurdity of this situation was so flagrant that he got the system changed. Hereditary peers are now free to renounce their peerage and sit in the Commons. Sir Alec Douglas-Home and Anthony Lambton have taken advantage of this privilege. Up till 1911 there was no legal limit to the power of the House of Lords except that it was accepted that the final control of taxation rested with the Commons. No bill could be put on the Statute Book if the Lords remained obstinate in their refusal to pass it. But when the Liberals came back to power in 1906 with an overwhelming majority the Lords broke with the tradition of the Duke of Wellington (see p. 50) and rejected Liberal measure after Liberal measure although there was no reason at all to think that those measures in any way misrepresented the will of the electorate. Balfour threw out the reckless and revolutionary challenge that 'it was the duty of everyone to see the Unionist party should still control, whether in power or whether in opposition, the destinies of this great Empire'—in power through the Commons, in opposition through the Lords. It was a challenge which the Government could hardly avoid taking up and when the Lords threw out Lloyd George's budget it was left with no alternative.

An election was held in January 1910, and when that election returned the Liberal Government again to power, though with a much reduced majority and dependent now on the votes of the Irish Nationalists, the Lords gave way and passed the budget. But Irish Home Rule still remained. The Irish naturally insisted on this as the price of their continued support. The Lords with their absentee Irish landlords were as adamant in their opposition. When a compromise could not be reached, the Liberal Government requested the new King, George V, on the precedent of the Treaty of Utrecht, to agree, if necessary, to the creation of a sufficient number of new peers to carry the measure. The King with great reluctance gave the promise, though only if the Government was sustained by a new election. That new election was held in November 1910 and gave almost exactly the same result as that of the early months of the year. The Government then passed through the Commons its bill making it possible for a bill to become law without acceptance of the House of Lords, if it was passed three times through the Commons. The Lords passed this by 131 votes to 114, moderate Conservatives like Lord Curzon following the precedent set by the Duke of Wellington eighty years before, the die-hards maintaining their opposition to the end. The King was thus saved from the unwelcome necessity of creating new peers. The Lords continued in their opposition to the Home Rule Bill but it was now possible to carry that bill over their veto by invoking the provisions of the Parliament Act. It was the Irish who brought the issue of the Lords' veto to a head.

Recent years have brought three new developments in the situation of the Lords. A new Parliament Act of 1949 has substituted two passages through the House of Commons for three as the condition of putting on the Statute Book an Act which has not received the Lords' assent; in 1958 the creation of life peerages was at last accepted, and, though the hereditary peers still keep their seats, it seems unlikely that any other than life peerages will ever be created again; and, the same year, women peers were admitted.

As a result of the creation of life peers, the Lords are today a less overwhelmingly Conservative body than in the past. In the 1968 Parliament 125 Members took the Conservative whip as against 95 who took the Labour. The chance of the Lords calling up the back-woods peers to vote down a Labour Government is not now perhaps very large. They are well aware that if they did so they would sign their own death warrant. Still, the fear of such a thing happening has a certain influence over Labour thinkers.

The preamble to the Parliament Act of 1911 states that 'it is intended to substitute for the House of Lords as it at present exists a Second Chamber constituted on a popular rather than a hereditary basis'. The present House of Lords is indeed an anomaly, being the only hereditary Chamber surviving anywhere in the world, and a number of attempts have been made to carry out the promise of the Parliament Act—notably a Commission which sat under Lord Bryce during the First World War. But all have ended in failure. The truth is that Labour and left-wing opinion has little appetite for a radical reform of the House of Lords. Some, though not most, would abolish it altogether. But, if it must survive, it is from the left-wing point of view, desirable that it should be as anomalous and illogical as possible. From such a body a Labour majority in the Commons has little to fear. A House of Lords 'constituted on a popular basis' might be a rival to the House of Commons as the American Senate is a rival to the House of Representatives. Therefore in 1968, when they at last came to wrestle with the problem, the leaders of the three parties agreed to recommend not a popular Chamber but a Chamber nominated by themselves. Rather to their own surprise they found that their plan encountered violent opposition from back-benchers on both sides who perhaps did not so greatly care how the House of Lords was constituted as resent its whole constitution being arranged in hugger-mugger fashion between the party leaders. Mr. Wilson who was not perhaps greatly interested in the project, in view of the opposition with which it was meeting and, grudging the time that its passage would take, dropped it. The whole episode is perhaps the most notable example since the war that the back-benchers cannot be always and totally treated as the mere lobby-fodder of their leaders.

The House of Lords differs from the Commons in its provision of cross benches. In the Parliament of 1968 out of 241 frequent attenders 52 sat on the cross benches. The cross-benchers are often people who have had wide experience of life in some field other than that of party politics. Owing to them and owing to the fact that they have no constituents to pacify party discipline is a great deal less rigid than in the Commons. If we go back a hundred or a hundred and fifty years, a very high proportion of the members of every Cabinet were Lords. Now the Commons and public opinion resent it if an important minister is not available to be questioned in the Commons and ministers in the Lords are less frequent. Every Cabinet has at least two, the Lord Chancellor and the Leader of the House. In some modern Cabinets there have been more. There are always a number of junior ministers whose task it is to answer questions. There is a steady flow of Members from the Commons to the Lords, as Members of the Commons, usually senior and retiring Members, become ennobled. A danger of the system of creation of life peers is that people are not likely to be made life peers until they have attained a fairly advanced age. Therefore a House that consists only of life peers is likely to be a very elderly body. If we are to look on it merely as a delaying body, that perhaps does not greatly matter. After all a Senate, by its very name, implies old age. But those who think that the Lords could and should have a more positive role and contribute independent opinions to the wisdom of the national policies may regret a total absence of the young.

The resolutions of the Parliament Acts do not wholly deprive the Lords of power. They still have, if they care to exercise it, power over delegated legislation; statutory instruments requiring affirmative or negative resolutions can, unless they are financial, be rejected by a resolution of the House of Lords. The only occasion when the Lords have ventured to use that power was in June 1968 when they rejected an order giving effect to a resolution of the United Nations to apply sanctions to Rhodesia. Their vote was however no more than a gesture as when a similar order was again introduced they passed it.

It was a vote of the Lords which prevented the new clause for the abolition of capital punishment from reaching the Statute Book in 1948. The Government could of course have passed the clause again through the Commons and overridden the Lords' veto. But the clause had originally been inserted not by the Government but by a free vote and public opinion, as was judged at the time, was strongly opposed to abolition. The Government of the day—the Labour Government—was therefore not willing to take issue with the Lords on such a point any more than Gladstone's Government had been willing to take issue with the Lords over his Home Rule Bill, and capital punishment was for the moment maintained.

It is the law that money bills should be introduced first in the Commons, and the Government also introduces in the Commons any bills that are highly controversial or of major importance. But it is often convenient to introduce minor bills into the Lords. If they contain incidental financial provisions the Lords send the bill to the Commons with the financial words printed in brackets and underlined so as to call the attention of the Commons to the fact that the Lords are not claiming to have passed those words.

In the Lords there are often interesting debates, made the more interesting by the speakers of widely different experience speaking untrammelled by party discipline. But the main legislative task of the Lords is as a revising body with a duty to tidy up hasty drafting when such is to be found, as it often is, in the bills as they have left the Commons. In the pressure of modern life such a revising body is essential and if the House of Lords were to be abolished some other body to take its place would certainly have to be invented.

The House of Lords is not only a House of Parliament but also a Court of Law. It is only with its former function that we are here primarily concerned. The judicial functions of the Lords are of great antiquity and date back to the days when it was the King's Great Council, and to the demand of Magna Carta that a man should be tried by his peers. During the fifteenth and sixteenth centuries they were practically dormant. In the eighteenth century they were exercised by the Lord Chancellor who was attended only by two other silent peers to represent the rest of the House. Towards the end of the nineteenth century Lord Selborne proposed a general reform of the legal system which would have had the effect of robbing the House of Lords of its judicial function. But an Act of 1876 restored to it these functions and appointed salaried Lords of Appeal to perform them. By that act no appeal can be heard by the Lords unless three persons with special legal qualifications are present to hear it. Nominally it is the whole House which is the court. No law forbids peers without legal qualifications from sitting in the court, but they never do so and what would happen if they attempted to do so is uncertain.

Beside being a general Court of Appeal the Lords have had three judicial functions. They have had to judge in cases of impeachment, in the trial of peers and in peerage disputes. Impeachment of course played a large part in the life of the past. In the days when the minister was still really the King's minister, impeachment was the way in which Parliament could get rid of an unpopular minister. It was thus for instance that Parliament was able to strike down the ministers of the seventeenth century, although against Strafford a special Act of Attainder had to be invoked. The machinery of impeachment was used against Warren Hastings and was used for the last time against Pitt's colleague, Dundas, in 1806. In modern custom there is no need for such a procedure, as the House of Commons can more easily dismiss a minister by passing a vote of censure on him.

Peers had the right of trial before their peers if charged with felony or treason. The occasion has only occurred rarely and was last used with Lord Clifford in 1935. By the Criminal Justice Act of 1948 the privilege of peers in criminal cases was abolished.

If a peerage is in dispute or has fallen into abeyance and a claimant wishes to recall it, the Crown refers the matter to the Lords and the Lords hand over the task of investigating it to the Committee of Privileges.

2

The House of Commons: The Length of Parliament's Life

Other countries—most notably the United States—have their elections at fixed dates over which the executive has no control. Such has never been the British custom. Before the Civil War a King who was at loggerheads with public opinion only summoned a Parliament when he was compelled to do so by the need of money. Both James I and Charles I ruled for long periods without a Parliament. Nor was there any settled time for the life of a single Parliament. After the Revolution of 1688 this was altered and in order to keep Parliament in touch with its electorate, no Parliament, it was ordained, was to last more than three years before a fresh election. With George I's accession, however, the Whig masters feared that Parliament and electorate might be too closely in touch. They feared that public opinion, hostile to the Act of Settlement which had put the Hanovers on the throne, might be running in a Tory and Jacobite direction; and therefore, to avoid an immediate election, they altered the length of a Parliament from three years to seven, and the Septennial Act, which remained until modern times, was passed. It was only in 1911 that the period was changed from seven years to five. But Parliament, according to the British system, is omnicompetent: it is free to settle the length of its own life and may at any time change its own arrangements. During both the two World Wars it was not thought advisable to have an election while the war was going on and therefore the life of Parliament was prolonged until the fighting ceased. The Parliament of 1910 thus went on until 1918 and that of 1935 until 1945. Even according to the regular legislation the seven years, so long as the Septennial Act remained in force, and the five years of today, are merely maximum periods. The election does not as in America automatically take place on the day that the five years are up. The Sovereign can dissolve Parliament and call for an election at any time and the Sovereign of course, acts on the advice of the Prime Minister. The Prime Minister may at any time call for an election if the affairs of the country and party allegiances have fallen into irreparable confusion, as happened in 1931 after the formation of the National Government. Apart from that, it is usual for a Prime Minister to select a date most to his own convenience—a date usually a little before the full date of the Parliament's life.

This power of choice gives a considerable advantage to the Prime Minister and the party in power over the Opposition, and in modern times an advantage even larger than previously. Before the War of 1914 we lived under a gold standard which the legislators generally regarded as unchallengeable. The Government did not think that it could do anything to control the trade cycle. Today the Keynesian techniques have put a new power into the hand of the Government. It is possible to expand or contract the economy at choice and, however much larger forces may be responsible for longer-term prosperity or adversity, it is not difficult by policies of inflation to create a condition of immediately abundant money and apparent prosperity. It is easily possible to make everybody prosperous on Election Day, even though perhaps they may have to pay for it on the day after, and it is the general habit of the Chancellor of the Exchequer of both parties to do this. So common is the trick, so great the advantage which it brings to the reigning Government, that until recently it was often said that it was no longer possible to beat a Government at an election. Such was common talk in 1970. The Labour Government had before that election for some time steadily run behind the Conservatives in the polls and at bye-elections. Then towards Easter the polls took a turn in Labour's favour.

Mr. Wilson thought that if he took advantage of that moment he could win an election. He went to the country. His victory was generally predicted, but, greatly to most people's surprise—and not least to his own—he was defeated.

Whatever the rights or wrongs of the 1970 election, it has at least proved that a reigning Government is not invariably unbeatable. Yet the advantages which the Executive has in its ability to rig matters both financially and in other ways is certainly very great and it is a commonplace of warning among the pollsters that they expect their figures to move a few points in favour of a Government when an election takes place. In consequence a number of critics—Mr. Ronald Butt, Mr. Ian Gilmour and Mr. Roger Fulford for instance—afraid of the excessive dominance of the Executive over the Legislature in modern times, have suggested, in letters to *The Times*, that it would be a good plan to deprive the Prime Minister of his advantage by fixing a definite date for elections quite outside his control. It is also argued that the power to threaten a dissolution gives to the Prime Minister a potent weapon with which to discipline discontent within his own party. He can always threaten the rebels with a general election and it is argued that this weapon makes him too powerful. But as to that, though such a threat may sometimes be used, it is unlikely to be used very often: for a Prime Minister who went to the country with his party divided behind him would not be likely to do very well at the election and would in all probability be inviting his own defeat. Yet there is a good deal to be said for the general argument for fixed dates for elections. The practical obstacle to its implementation is the same as the obstacle to proportional representation, or any other plan for giving a fairer deal to the minority. It is always the minority that favours such plans and naturally the majority are less keen on them. The Government, whatever Government it be, does not find anything gravely amiss with a system that gives it an advantage. The Liberals today call for proportional representation. They said little about such devices before 1914 when they could get themselves elected without them.

The use of the referendum is another case in point. In the controversies about our entry into the Common Market there was a lot of discussion whether the issue should be submitted to a referendum. Mr. Heath rejected the suggestion. He said that it is not our British tradition—that the verdict should be given by Parliament. It is indeed our British tradition that the verdict should be given by Parliament, and had Mr. Heath not given a perhaps ill-considered promise that he would not take the country in without the 'full-hearted consent of Parliament and the people', there would perhaps have been little cause for argument. Certainly the general opinion of the habit of the British people, in contradiction to that of some other people, has induced a wariness of referenda. At the time when the House of Commons voted for the abolition of capital punishment there were some who argued that all the evidence showed that public opinion was opposed to abolition—as it undoubtedly was; and some said that the public should be allowed to express its opinion through a referendum. But it was fairly convincingly answered that there was good reason to think that public opinion has always been opposed to every measure of penal reform, and that had the matter been settled by referenda we might still be hanging little children for stealing a few feet of silk. It was, we were told, for Parliament to lead the way and, when it led wisely, public opinion came afterwards to endorse its leadership, even if it was not ready for it at the moment. There was sound force in such reasoning. But when Mr. Heath went on to maintain that the referendum has never played a part in British political life he a little exaggerated. When the restriction of the powers of the House of Lords was at issue before the First World War it was Balfour, as a Conservative leader, who suggested that the question should be submitted to a referendum—'to that great democratic engine', as he described it, 'employed by almost all countries, which every other country but our own enjoys'. The Government refused. Left-wing opinion has never accepted a referendum in this country whatever it may have done elsewhere. But there is a Conservative precedent for its advocacy. Perhaps it is not really so much a matter of left-wing and right-wing but rather that, as with proportional representation, those who are winning in Parliament are against it and those who are losing in Parliament are in favour of it.

The life of a Parliament is divided into sessions. The Sovereign in her proclamation for a general election appoints a date for voting and also a date for the meeting of the new Parliament. On that date the new Parliament is opened by a Speech from the Throne in which the ministers cause the Sovereign to announce the measures that are proposed for the coming first session of the new Parliament. It is within the power of the Prime Minister to tailor the dates of a session. Since legislation that has not been completed by the end of a session is wiped out and has to begin again from the beginning in the next session, it is often convenient for Parliament after the summer recess to attach a few days to the old session in order to round off uncompleted legislation. Special arrangements are normally made by which uncompleted private bills are carried over from the one session to the next to save the promoters expense. At the general holiday times throughout the year—Easter, Whitsuntide, Christmas and the summer recess—the House adjourns. When the House proceeds from one session to the next shortly after its return from its summer holiday the House is said to be prorogued. During a period of adjournment the Speaker and the Lord Chancellor on the request of the Prime Minister can recall Parliament in the event of a crisis demanding its attention, as happened at the Czechoslovak crisis in 1968.

3

The House of Commons: Conditions of Membership

Members of Parliament in the Middle Ages were paid by their constituents. In the seventeenth century as Parliament became more important and powerful it was found no longer necessary to pay men to go to it and the last Member to receive a regular salary from his constituents was the poet Andrew Marvell who was the Member for Hull in Charles II's reign; in return for a subvention, he furnished his constituents with a regular report on the affairs of the nation. After him in the eighteenth century Members were of course anxious enough to be paid by being appointed to salaried sinecure posts, but they were not directly paid merely for being Members either by the Treasury or by their constituents. In the nineteenth century the Irish Nationalists used to be paid out of party funds, but there was no direct Treasury payment to Members until 1911. So in fact before that—and indeed afterwards—it was very difficult for a man wholly without means to go into Parliament. But the formal disqualifications on membership were throughout all modern times few. The requirement of a property qualification had long fallen into abeyance and was formally abolished by Act of Parliament in 1858. The religious disqualifications against Catholics, Jews and Nonconformists were all abolished during the nineteenth century. (No religious disqualification survives, though whether a Catholic can be Lord Chancellor is a question that has not been put to the test.) The only disqualifications were fairly self-evident ones. A lunatic, a peer, an undischarged bankrupt and a convicted traitor were excluded. No one could be a Member who was under twenty-one years of age, although in the eighteenth century this disqualification was often disregarded. A most notable example was Charles James Fox who both sat for Midhurst and spoke before he was of age. The law by the various Reform Bills regulated fairly rigidly who could vote for Parliament. It was not very rigid about who could sit in it. There was no requirement, as there was in America, that a Member had to reside in his constituency. Some constituencies have demanded residence of their Member. But that was a private arrangement or demand and many of the most distinguished of Parliamentarians, notably Winston Churchill, during the course of their careers travelled round the country and stood for a variety of constituencies with which they had no personal connection. The most debatable disqualification for membership throughout the ages was that of women. Women Abbesses, as we have seen, had sat in the House of Lords in the Middle Ages, but apart from this, no woman had ever been allowed to vote for or to sit in Parliament. The Parliament (Qualification of Women) Act of 1918 removed that disability. A number of women stood at the General Election of that year but none in Britain was elected. The only woman elected was the Sinn Feiner, the Countess Markiewicz, who, like other Sinn Feiners did not take her seat. The first woman to be returned to Westminster was Lady Astor in 1919. The first woman to hold a Government position was Margaret Bondfield in Ramsay Macdonald's Labour Government. Women were still excluded from the House of Lords until the passing of the Life Peerages Act in 1957. The first life peeress was appointed in 1958.

Like most of the institutions of British history, the British constitution was the consequence of accident rather than of design. We are often told—and rightly told —that the great difference between the American and the British constitution is that in this country the ministers sit in Parliament of which they are Members, and in America they are not allowed to belong to the legislature. In neither country was that the product of design. In America before independence the States, or colonies as they then were, all had their own legislatures. Their power was limited, however. The Governors, just as in the seventeenth century the ministers in England, were the ministers of the King and not of Parliament. Therefore after independence it was thought natural and desirable to continue this system. Governors were no longer sent out from England, they were elected by the people on the spot; but they were elected separately from the legislature, and the Executive and the legislature were left to fight out their differences as best they might. To the contrary in England after the Civil War it was not at once settled that the ministers should be the ministers of Parliament rather than of the King. Throughout Charles II's reign it was still uncertain where real power rested. It was for a time suggested that office-holders should be excluded from Parliament. The suggestion had been made to forestall a possible revival of the King's power against Parliament. Had that design established itself we must necessarily have evolved a system not unlike the American. It did not succeed in its full purpose. By the Act of Settlement of 1701 all ministers were, as in the American manner, excluded from sitting in the Commons. The inconvenience of that separation was soon recognised, so by the amended Act of 1707, the Statute of Anne, as it is called, ministers were allowed to sit but compelled, on their appointment, to submit themselves for re-election. Thereafter up till very modern times—up till 1919—anyone who accepted ministerial office under the Crown had still to resign his seat, though he was allowed to stand for re-election. The necessity was a most profound nuisance to new recipients of office. It was defended as a good way by which public opinion could express its favour or disfavour towards Government policies, and there were some statesmen of whom Mr. Masterman just before the 1914 War was the chief, who were plagued with misfortune and lost bye-election after bye-election on their appointment to office, until eventually they had to retire in despair from public life. The obligation was only removed by the Re-election of Ministers Act of 1919. Apart from ministerial office, appointment to an 'office of profit under the Crown' still disqualifies a person from sitting in the House of Commons. Such offices are listed in the House of Commons Disqualification Act, 1957, which is revised from time to time.

To this day a Member cannot resign his seat at Westminster. He vacates it only by accepting one or other of a number of totally non-existent posts—Steward of the Chiltern Hundreds, or Steward of the Manor of Northstead.

4

The House of Commons: Its Privileges, Rules and Discipline

The members of a sovereign legislative body must necessarily have certain privileges to enable them to do their work freely. If we go back to Henry VIII's time we find that these privileges were reasonably observed when the King's interests were not directly challenged, as when he allowed Parliament under Sir Thomas More's Speakership to refuse Wolsey a subsidy for his French War. However when he was directly challenged, Henry's reaction was very different. 'Ho, man,' he shouted at Edward Montague when there was delay about the passage of the bill for the suppression of the lesser monasteries, 'will they suffer my bill to pass? Get my bill forward by tomorrow or else tomorrow this head of yours will be off.' In Elizabeth's time the Puritan criticism of the monarchy began to show itself. 'We are none of us without fault, not even our noble Queen,' said Wentworth the Puritan. They clapped him in the Tower but Elizabeth had the sense to release him. Yet it was, as we should naturally expect, in the seventeenth century that the rights of the Members of Parliament, by which they were to protect themselves against the coercion of the King, were codified. In 1629 a judgement was obtained in the courts against Sir John

Eliot, Denzil Holles and Benjamin Valentine for their speeches and conduct in Parliament. This verdict was in 1641 fully repudiated upon a writ of error by the House of Lords. The privileges of Members of Parliament were specifically asserted by the Bill of Rights of 1688 which granted them freedom of speech and freedom from arrest. This protection, ruled a Committee of the Commons, 'extended to everything said or done by a Member in performance of his duties as a Member in a committee of the House or a joint committee of both Houses as well as everything said or done by him in the House in the trans-action of parliamentary business'. This protection for Members was reaffirmed in the Parliamentary Privileges Act of 1770. A Member cannot be sued for slander for any words spoken in the chamber. The freedom from arrest only applied to arrest in civil proceedings and since imprisonment in civil process has now been virtually abolished this privilege is no longer of great importance. Privilege is derived from the concessions granted to Members by the royal assent to the Bill of Rights and the first task of every newly elected Speaker is to ask of the Sovereign, or of the Lord Chancellor as his representative, the confirmation for the Commons of 'their ancient and undoubted rights and privileges'. The reply is that Her Majesty 'most readily confirms all the rights and privileges which have ever been granted or conferred upon the Commons by Her Majesty or any of her royal predecessors'.

The general proposition that legislators should be free is self-evident. The question how far and how often it is desirable to invoke privileges is more debatable. A case for instance could well be made out that there is an interfer-ence with freedom if a Whip seeks to direct a Member into one division lobby rather than another—still more so if, as was done until recently and was certainly still done when I was in the House after 1945, a Whip seats himself at the exit from the central lobby and attempts to dissuade or to prevent Members from leaving the House. Where do attempts of pressure groups to persuade a Member to vote a certain way become a breach of privilege?

In July 1947, the House of Commons on the motion of W. J. Brown, the Independent Member for Rugby, passed with the support of many Labour Members a motion that 'it is inconsistent with the dignity of the House, with the duty of a Member to his constituents and with the maintenance of the privilege of freedom of speech for any particular Member of this House to enter into any contractual agreement with an outside body controlling or limiting the Member's complete freedom of action in Parliament or stipulating that he will act in any way as the representative of such outside body in regard to any matter to be transacted in Parliament'. This principle played a considerable part in the controversy whether Labour Members who supported our entry into the European Common Market should be in any way compelled to act against it at the dictate of the majority of the party conference.

From time to time Members raise as a matter of privilege complaints that have been made about the general conduct or standard of Members. For instance shortly after the 1945 election a new Labour Member, Mr. Garry Alligham, complained of the prevalence of drunkenness among Members. Ten years later the editor of a Sunday newspaper, *The Sunday Express*, was summoned to the bar of the House for rebuke for having alleged that Members used their position to get for themselves improper favours in petrol rationing. Indeed among the newly arrived Labour Members after 1945 were some who were unduly sensitive in resenting alleged violations of their privileges. 'During the two Parliaments since 1945,' wrote *The Times* on August 1, 1951, 'and particularly during the last year, more and more Members of the House of Commons have sought to use privilege as a weapon by which to restrict the free discussion of political issues. This is no new danger. Parliamentary Government means government by a majority and there is always a danger that the majority may be oppressive. Significantly it is Labour Members of Parliament who, since their party was returned with a majority in 1945, have been most active in bringing complaints of breach of privilege against members of the general public. The threat to liberty may not for the moment seem great but this does not lessen the need for vigilance. As has been apparent during the past year, sensitivity to public criticism is an infectious disease; one complaint of breach of privilege encourages another. "It is undesirable," said the Committee of Privileges earlier this year, "to restrict the freedom of discussion unduly." Members of Parliament should recall these words before they seek refuge from the harsh winds of public criticism behind the obsolete claims of Parliamentary privilege.'

Happily Members, Labour Members and others, paid attention to these warnings and in recent years there has been a much greater reluctance to invoke the protection of privilege.

It is of the essence of Parliamentary sovereignty that Parliament should make for itself its own rules. In the Middle Ages it was the King who summoned Parliament at his will. In Tudor times it was again the Sovereign who created constituencies to serve his pleasure. Since full establishment of Parliamentary sovereignty with the Hanoverians it is Parliament which has made its own rules for itself. It makes the rules of its own elections. When a seat is vacant it is the House of Commons which issues the writ for the new election. This writ is usually moved by the Chief Whip of the party to which the late Member belonged. It is understood that the Chief Whip has freedom within reason to choose the time for the new bye-election that best suits his party's interest, but, if he delays beyond all decency, it is open to another Member to move the writ. During a recess or adjournment the Speaker can put in train the machinery for a new election by his own act. In 1604 the House established the right to decide for itself disputed elections. At first it remitted such cases to a Committee of Privileges but in the eighteenth century these cases were fought out before a Committee of the Whole House. The decisions that emerged from these debates were so flagrantly partisan and scandalous that in 1800, by the Parliamentary Elections Act, they were remitted to two judges of the High Court.

The House has also the right to expel a Member whom it deems unfit. The two famous victims of such a process were John Wilkes and Charles Bradlaugh. Wilkes on his election for Middlesex in 1764 was barred from the House for having published 'a false, scandalous and seditious libel'. But at new elections his constituents persisted in returning him until in 1782 the House gave way and allowed him to take his seat. Bradlaugh was a professed atheist who announced that if he took the oath he considered its invocation of divine assistance to be meaningless. He, too, when expelled, was re-elected by his constituents of Northampton at the bye-election and was allowed to sit, it being decided that a Member, if he wished, could make an affirmation in place of taking an oath.

Whatever may have been done at various periods of history, Parliament now considered it as one of its main businesses to see to it that no Member derives any improper financial advantage from his membership. No Member who has a direct financial interest in a matter is allowed to vote on it. If he has merely a general interest in a proposition of public interest which is being discussed he is not indeed debarred from voting but he has to declare his interest. In this he is more strictly disciplined than the Member of the House of Lords, who does not have to make a direct declaration but is expected not to speak or vote on matters that are to his financial advantage 'on his honour'.

In modern times the habit has grown up of public relations bodies and other such institutions employing Members for a salary or fee to promote their interests. It is not forbidden for a Member to accept such commissions, but there are obviously both difficulties and dangers in the growth of the habit, and a select Committee on the declaration of Members' interests considered the whole problem in 1969. It was particularly concerned if a Member was in receipt of payments from a foreign government. However, no changes have been made in existing practice.

It is forbidden for a private Member to propose any new Government expenditure. The proposal of such expenditure is reserved to ministers. The private Member can only propose a reduction. This is considered to be a guarantee against crude corruption, such as Members voting themselves money, and no doubt in this it is effective. Whether because of specific regulations or because of the general standard of honour in Parliamentary life no one doubts that today crude bribery in the sense of Members selling their votes is unknown. I remember when I was a Member a curious Conservative one day saying quite casually, 'I wonder if some of those Labour fellows would object if I offered them a couple of quid to pair with me.' He had no more tendentious ambition than to get early to bed and it had not occurred to him that the proposal might seem to savour of corruption and would be likely to be resented. However he was easily laughed off from making it.

Ministers are naturally under much stricter discipline than private Members. A minister on assuming office is required to resign any directorships that he may hold and to sell his shares in any company which may in any way be involved with his public duties, and to avoid the use of any knowledge which he has acquired as a minister to procure shares for himself. The most recent guidance laid down in 1952 states that 'a minister must so order his affairs that no conflict arises between his private interests and his public duties'. This guidance was a mere restatement of the traditional ruling. The major case in modern times when ministerial conduct was called in question was over the Marconi case just before the First World War. Wireless telegraphy was then in its infancy and the Government decided to take over the British Marconi Company. It was discovered that, after the Government's decision had been taken but before it had been published, two ministers of the day, Rufus Isaacs, afterwards Lord Reading, and Lloyd George, had bought Marconi shares.

They denied that they had bought any shares in *the* Company—that is, the British Marconi Company—and this was true—but they had bought and concealed shares in the American Marconi Company, shares which at that time stood very low but which were likely to benefit by the advertisement to Marconi given by the British Government's acquisition of the British company. A select committee was set up to investigate the case and, although it gave its verdict on strictly party lines, the Liberals all voting for the ministers and the Conservatives voting against them, it was generally felt that the ministers had behaved perhaps not with corruption but with extreme indiscretion. During the First World War and immediately after it, under Lloyd George's premiership, the sale of honours is generally thought to have become scandalously common, but these practices were suppressed under Baldwin when he became Prime Minister and have never since been widely resorted to. In more recent times the rules to which ministers have submitted have been extremely strict. In 1935 it was discovered that J. H. Thomas, then a member of the Cabinet, had revealed secrets of the forthcoming budget, and he was compelled not merely to resign from the Cabinet but to leave public life altogether. Attlee after the Second World War was extremely rigorous in such matters. An under-secretary, John Belcher, was found to have had unhealthily close relations with a shady adventurer, a Mr. Stanley. The matter was submitted to a tribunal, the Lynskey Tribunal, and Belcher was compelled to leave public life. Even harsher treatment was dealt out by Attlee to his Chancellor of the Exchequer, Hugh Dalton. Dalton made an indiscreet remark to a journalist in the lobby about a proposal which he had included in the budget which he was about to present. He thought nothing of it but the journalist, sensing a scoop, put it in his paper before its public announcement. No particular harm was done but Dalton resigned.

Of course it is often said that the best remedy against corruption is to see to it that Members are adequately paid.

It cannot be pretended that in history, whether in Britain or in any other country, whether among politicians or elsewhere, rich men have not often been found to use devious means for making themselves still richer. Nevertheless the general proposition is obviously true. Whether to prevent corruption or out of general justice those who are paid should be paid adequately. From Andrew Marvell's time up till 1911 Members of Parliament, as has been said, were not officially paid for being Members. In the eighteenth century there were a number of sinecure posts with salaries attached to them and influential Members were able to get themselves appointed to these. After the Reform Bill the civil service was greatly regularised. It was then no longer possible for a civil servant to be a Member of Parliament, and the opportunities for sinecure jobs were greatly reduced. Members had to live on their own incomes to a much greater extent than previously. On the other hand with the growth in the national wealth owing to the industrial revolution the number of persons possessed of an independent income was greatly increased.

If it is desired to have an aristocratic society, it is possible to ask members of that aristocracy and wealthy persons to perform public work without any direct remuneration, but obviously such a system means that those who are without means are effectively excluded from public life. Before 1886 this was thought no handicap. There was one obvious consequence of the extension of the franchise so as to give virtually universal manhood suffrage: with the passage of time, the unmoneyed began to argue that the privilege of franchise was not of much use to them if they could never send one of themselves to Parliament. In 1911 it was decided to pay a salary of £400 a year to a Member of Parliament. In 1937 that salary was raised from £400 to £600. The sums were not, and were not intended to be, princely. They were merely sufficient to make it possible for any desirable person to go into Parliament. As Neville Chamberlain put it in introducing the 1937 vote, the salary was 'not so high that it becomes an inducement to people to enter the House for the purpose of earning more than they would outside, and not so low that men or women who could give valuable service to the House should be prevented from doing so merely by the fact that they had not sufficient means'. With rising prices the Members' salaries have in post-war years been raised again on four more occasions until they at present stand at about £4,000. Members also get certain incidental allowances. They can claim up to £1,000 for secretarial expenses. They get free rail or air travel between London and their constituencies. Their wives can travel free to London a certain number of times a year. They receive the services of the library staff and so on.

Yet when all is said, figures adequately show that the remuneration and perquisites of British Members of Parliament compare unfavourably with those in other comparable countries. In particular the British Member gets far less adequate facilities in which to work. Recently something has been done to provide the ordinary Member with office facilities, and there is at present a scheme for building him further office accommodation across the road by Westminster Underground station. Until a few years ago he had to dictate his letters to his secretary perched on a seat in the corridors as best he could. The contrast to the spacious offices and services at the disposal of the American legislator was, and still is, most outstanding. It is true that in such a contrast we are not quite comparing like with like. The American legislator represents a much larger number of constituents than the British, and he is expected to do much more for them. American constituents look to their Congressmen and to their Senators for direct services that in Britain would be thought undesirable favours, and the British citizen gets his grievances remedied through the machinery of the civil service on many matters for which the American will go to his legislator. Still, when all is said, the disparity between the British and the American politician is enormous. Almost as great is the disparity between the British and the politician of many other countries which are not notably more prosperous than Britain.

Once we had moved to a society that no longer pretended to be aristocratic, the case for paying Members was unanswerable and, if they have to be paid, they should be paid sufficiently to give them no excuse for adding to their incomes in less reputable ways. Some ways of earning more money are easily compatible with Membership of the House of Commons. A barrister can combine the two jobs, though with certain difficulties. A Member can sit on a board of a company and many companies like to have a Member on their board. He who has a talent for journalism can always write. He who has the gift of broadcasting is more likely to get broadcasting work if he is a Member of Parliament than if he is not. But, though there is no reason why a Member should not add to his income in such fortuitous ways, it would be highly undesirable that he should be entirely dependent on these pickings, and there are some jobs—that of the manual worker for instance—which it would be quite impossible to combine with Membership. If he did not receive a general salary, a Member of that type would get no income at all. It is true that the Trade Union Member usually receives some subvention from his union. The habit is understandable and legitimate. But if we remember W. J. Brown's case (see p. 68) we cannot doubt that it has its dangers, just as membership of a directorial board has its dangers. Both Trade Unions and companies like to get their money's worth for the price that they pay. Their methods are doubtless not methods of crude command but they are nonetheless real and usually effective.

If it be agreed that the Member should be paid, it obviously follows that in a time of inflation and rising prices his salary should go up with the increasing cost of living. Critics like Mr. George Schwartz of *The Sunday Times*, argue that if there has been inflation that is because of the negligence of Members of Parliament whose duty it was to prevent it. There was, he said, no reason why they should be rewarded for their failure of duty. But it is not an argument that seriously holds water. Whatever ought to be the case, whatever may be the case in theory, no one can pretend that in reality a back-bench Member of Parliament has sufficient control over the Government's financial policy to make it fair that he should be punished in his pocket if that policy is a failure. Yet even if we grant that with rising prices Members' salaries ought to be adjusted, there are the practical problems to which Members are often strangely insensitive. Who is to adjust them? Necessarily, through whatever machinery, in the last resort it is the House of Commons. No one else can adjust them. Now it is certainly true that the average member of the public little understands what are the calls on the purse of a Member of Parliament. Even after the recent revision, a Member of Parliament, receiving £4,000 a year, is not a rich man. Most of them would be a great deal richer if they were not Members. But there is no way of persuading the man in the street, who merely looks at the overall figure, that a Member of Parliament is not rich. The issue, in a day of inflation when all are calling with some reason for pay increases, is not so much, should M.P.s' pay be raised as, should they put themselves at the head of the queue? If they do so can they reasonably expect restraint from other claimants?

In 1946, Members' pay was raised from £600 to £1,000. The great majority supported this rise. A few, of whom I was one, opposed it and we opposed it with the argument that it would make more difficult the task of the Government in opposing inflation. There were further rises in 1954, 1957 and 1964 and a very steep one early in 1972—at a time when the containment of wage demands of every sort of worker was the main plank in the Government's programme. It is true that the increase was on the recommendation of a review body to whom the Government had remitted the question. But the increase had to be, and was without opposition, voted to itself by the House of Commons. The fact that Parliament had so recently raised its own salaries played its incidental but important part in the successful demand of the miners for their own very large readjustment at the beginning of 1972.

5

The Selection of Candidates

Since Joseph Chamberlain's day the power of party organisation has steadily grown. Whether that has been on balance to the advantage of the country is a matter for debate; it is certainly a fact that it has happened. The back-bench Member today has little more than the freedom of uncertainty as to who is his master. Is it the Whips? Or his constituency organisation? It is his constituency organisation which selects him in the first place. No Whip or Central Office can force him on an unwilling constituency organisation. A selection committee of that organisation summons to appear before it a selected number of those who have offered themselves as candidates. The would-be candidate has to make a short speech expounding his policies. He has to submit himself to some questioning. In these days his wife often has also to show herself, and then the selectors make a choice as between the applicants. Their choice has later to be ratified by a general meeting of the association, but the selection of the selection committee is generally, though not quite always, supported. On what principles selection committees will make their choice is something that no one can ever foretell with any certainty. Sometimes such matters as religious persuasion will be dismissed by a committee as totally unimportant. In another constituency it may lose a candidate his selection. Casual matters such as clothes and appearance obviously weigh heavily with one selector; not at all with another. Some like a candidate who is prominent in the public eye and likely to be given a place in a Government. Others think that such a Member would be more likely to neglect their interests than one destined to remain firmly on the back bench. I heard once of a couple of committed politicians from London who travelled down to the final meeting of a selection committee in a provincial constituency from which they both hoped for adoption. Each went in and said his piece and they then had to wait together in a sitting-room of the inn while the selectors reached their verdict. They waited on and on for hour after hour until at last the agent made his appearance and apologised to them for the unconscionable delay. 'The truth was,' he said, 'that we had a very difficult decision to make. Six of us were for Mr. A and six were for Sir Herbert B. So we thought that the only fair thing to do was to select neither of you.'

But the candidate, once adopted and elected, predominantly on a party vote where the vast majority of electors vote for the standard-bearer of their party irrespective of his personality, goes up to Westminster to become a Member and there it is the Whips who give him his daily orders. His constituents may grumble at some of the things that the party does, but, so long as he obeys the party line, the Member is unlikely to get into very serious trouble with them. The plea that that was what the party decided is generally sufficient to stifle all criticism. After all, there is nothing that disgruntled supporters can do in the constituency except to run a rival candidate at the next election and the likely effect of that is merely to present the constituency to the candidate of the opposition party on a split vote—a remedy that from the complainants' point of view would be a great deal worse than the disease.

The constituents, of course, get their opportunity when the next election comes round. They are under no obligation to re-adopt a Member if they dislike the way in which he has represented them. The former Member, on his part, even if not officially re-adopted, is entitled, if he wishes, to stand as an independent. Constituency associations are largely self-appointed coteries and sometimes misrepresent local opinion. An occasional ex-Member, such as S. O. Davies in Merthyr Tydfil, may perhaps be elected against an official candidate. But such successes are rare. The greater number, like Mr. Nigel Nicolson when his association rejected him at Bournemouth, have no alternative but to drop out of parliamentary life.

6

The Member as Welfare Officer

There is no misunderstanding about it that a Member has a duty at Westminster to support the party ticket. Presumably in most cases nearly half his constituents at the election voted against him. He is not expected to pay attention to their preferences in the division lobby. On the other hand, he is expected to fight a personal battle for a justified pension and the like in his capacity of welfare officer, and many Members consider it a matter of great pride that they fight these battles irrespective of whether the constituent with a grievance is a supporter or not. Mr. Max Nicholson, in his plans for making Parliamentary control over the Executive more effective, would have the Member bother less with these tasks of welfare officer and give more time to serving on specialist committees and making himself better equipped in the intricate workings of the particular department of his speciality. Some Members no doubt would welcome such changes; many, I am sure, would not. Many do not believe that, whatever reforms may be introduced, the Executive either would, or perhaps even should, submit itself to any effective control by Parliament. Those of them who are ensconced on the back benches do not expect any real control over policies—very likely they recognise their incapacity to exercise such control, or, if they yearn for it, are doomed to frustration. Occasionally, indeed, some great scandal breaks out when Parliament has—and takes —the opportunity to speak for the nation, but those opportunities come rarely, but once or twice perhaps in a Parliament. Through the greater part of its days the House gets through its prearranged programme to a foregone conclusion in accordance with the directions of the two groups of Whips.

To many back-benchers the welfare work in the constituency—the weekly surgery as it is called—is the most attractive part of the life, alone reconciling them to the drudgery of Westminster. To what extent the surgery work benefits the Member on election day when he offers himself for re-election is doubtful. The statistics seem to show that those who have been in this sense 'good' Members do not do better on polling day than those who have neglected their constituencies. For voters do not vote out of gratitude and they are right not to do so. (Those who do vote out of gratitude are too few to upset the electoral balance to any notable degree.) But this welfare work is in itself fascinating. Many give themselves to it with enthusiasm for love of it. He would be rendering a poor service to Parliament who deprived Members of the opportunity of doing it. The House is often at its best in exposing a purely personal injustice, as in its debates when Miss Irene Savidge was wrongfully arrested by the police in the park.

The growing complexity of life and the lack of clear definition of the boundaries of authority carry with them dangers to the liberty of the individual. Every day's newspapers and every day's experiences bring their tale of complaints of citizens overwhelmed with the multiplicity of forms and regulations that hamper them in the doing of their daily business. Some of these perplexities are the result of their own stupidity. Some are genuine. Life is admittedly complicated and the ordinary man and woman is only anxious to go about his simple business with as little interference as possible. The whole scale of the grievance was trenchantly attacked shortly after the First World War by Lord Hewart in his *New Despotism*. Professor Keeton in his *Passing of Parliament* has in recent years taken up the attack and shown that things have by no means got better since Hewart's day. An attempt has been made to mitigate the evil in the last years by the appointment of an Ombudsman to protect the citizen against maladministration.

III

THE CHAMBER

1

Its Seating

What are the physical conditions under which the House of Commons does its business? They are in a number of ways highly peculiar and most unlike those of any other legislature in the world. As has been said, up till Edward VI's time the House of Commons had no regular meeting place. Usually it met in London but by no means always so. Only in Edward VI's reign was it given a regular meeting place, in what previously had been the royal chapel in the Palace of Westminster. It sat there on the site of what is now St. Stephen's Hall until the fire in 1834. The site was the site of the chapel. The Speaker's chair was where the High Altar had been. A screen, where the choir screen had stood in its ecclesiastical days, divided the chamber from the lobby. Over the course of the years the ecclesiastical nature of the building had been effectively obscured by the changes introduced by Sir Christopher Wren, to whom, in the fashion of his day, the Gothic architecture of the chapel was a barbarism.

A result of the Members' being thus seated was that, instead of sitting round in a hemicycle, they had to sit in two rows of benches facing one another, like the benches of the Decani and Cantores of the old chapel. Wren increased the accommodation by providing a further six rows behind the Speaker's chair to fill up the space between the opposing rows of benches. At the beginning of the nineteenth century, after the Union with Ireland, accommodation had to be found for an additional hundred Irish Members. Wyatt provided this accommodation by pulling down the walls of the old chapel which had been three feet thick and substituting walls which were only one foot thick.

In 1834 some workmen overfilled a stove with old wooden tallies and started a fire. The chamber was burnt down. It could have been rebuilt to some entirely different architectural plan, but it so happened that the period was one in which the Gothic revival was in fashion, and therefore the House of Commons decided to rebuild their chamber in a style that was to be 'Gothic and Elizabethan'. They advertised for an architect who could perform this task and, after a competition, awarded the contract to Barry. Barry employed Pugin as his clerk of works and Pugin imposed a much more definitely ecclesiastical character to the building than Barry had foreseen. The result was a chamber that had two wholly unique characteristics. First, it continued to group the Members face-to-face across a gangway; this favoured the development of the two-party system of which we have already spoken. Secondly, more remarkable and perhaps even more important, instead of providing seats and perhaps desks for every Member, as is done in most legislatures, the chamber was built purposely insufficient to accommodate at any one time more than two thirds of the Members. This is a deliberate and very strange deficiency. Barry's chamber had only 437 places for 658 Members. This defect was defended with the argument that it was not to be expected or desired that all the Members should spend all their time in the chamber. They had many other important tasks—serving on committees, attending to constituents and the like—and 437 places were amply sufficient for the number that would be likely to attend at the very great majority of debates. A smaller chamber, it was argued, was more likely to produce a desirable, conversational type of debate. After Barry's chamber had been destroyed by Hitler's bombs in 1941 the House sat in the House of Lords, the Lords moving to the King's Robing Room. The Lords' chamber was twelve feet nine inches longer than the destroyed chamber. I must confess that I never noticed, and I do not think that I ever heard anyone comment on, the fact. But the Commons' Select Committee on Rebuilding appointed in 1943 decided that the increased length had 'brought a notable diminution of intimacy'. There was debate whether the new chamber should be made slightly wider to include an extra bench, but it was in the end decided not to do this and the new chamber with its five rows of benches is of exactly the same dimensions as the old. Again as in Barry's chamber there were no cross-benches. The handful of Members belonging to neither major party now have to sit on whichever side they object to least. A Member can, if he wishes, seat himself beyond the bar, but if he does so he is not technically in the House and may on no account interrupt or in any other way take part in the proceedings in the House. The only increased accommodation permitted in the new chamber was in the visitors' galleries. Visitors are, of course, permitted to come in to listen to the debates. But naturally they may on no account intervene in the proceedings, nor may any Member in his speech make any reference to any visitor who may be present.

The Speaker sits in his chair, raised above the level of the ordinary Members. These are grouped before him in their two sides, the Government's supporters to his right, the Opposition to his left. A carpet divides the two sides with a strip at each side of it which a Member, in speaking, must on no account overstep. Should he do so, he is at once greeted with shouts of 'Order, Order'. The space between the two strips is thought to be the length of two swords and thus sufficient to prevent the Members from making any physical attack on one another. In front of the Speaker is the Clerk's table, on which are two Dispatch Boxes from one of which the Government front-bench speaker makes his speech, from the other, the Opposition front-bench speaker. Back-bench speakers have to make their speeches from the place where they have been sitting and from which they have risen to catch the Speaker's eye. On the Clerk's table is also the mace, the symbol that the House is in session. When the House goes into committee (see p. 104) the mace is removed and placed beneath the table.

It is argued that seats for two thirds of the Members are amply sufficient for all normal days. On especially exciting occasions Members crowd in, sit on one another's knees or perch in the gangways. The bustle creates what Churchill called 'a sense of crowd and urgency'. He pleaded successfully for a reproduction of all the oddities of the old chamber in the new. As it happened, in the 1945 Parliament the Labour majority was so large that there was never any question of a critical division which threatened the existence of the Government. The only division of importance of which the result was at all doubtful was that on the abolition of capital punishment. In subsequent Parliaments the differences between the parties have been much narrower and there have been a number of exciting, uncertain divisions. The most exciting have been those on our entry into the European Community, the outcome of which was often very doubtful, owing to the large revolts against the official party line among Members of both parties.

2

The Orders of the Day

Naturally modern developments have brought changes in Parliamentary procedure, the details of which will be later discussed. But it is remarkable not that these changes have taken place but that so much of the traditions of past centuries have been preserved into the present and very different age.

The hours of the House's meetings have changed considerably over the ages, the procedure of legislation surprisingly little. In Plantagenet times the House usually met for only a few days, passed its resolutions and then dispersed again. Regular continuous sittings only came in with the seventeenth century, and the House then usually sat from 8.30 or 9.00 in the morning. Artificial light was a problem, and a common method of obstruction for those who wanted to delay the House's business was to oppose the motion 'that candles be brought in'. During the electricians' dispute in 1970, for the first time for very many decades the House had to be lit by candle-light. In the eighteenth century, although on the motion for adjournment it was always voted that the House should adjourn until 9.00 the next morning, in fact it used not to meet until nearer 3.30 in the afternoon. The sittings then continued indefinitely through the night, though there was nothing of the modern Whip's coercion to keep Members there.

It was the penetration of the first rays of the morning sun which furnished Pitt with his famous Virgilian quotation on the abolition of the slave trade. In the nineteenth century with the development of the organised party system, which required of a Member a more regular attendance, and with Irish obstruction, late-night sittings became more burdensome. By the Standing Orders of 1888 it was ordained that the House should adjourn at midnight unless the rule was suspended. In 1906 the hour was moved back to 11.00. The old custom was that there should be an adjournment for a dinner hour—the Speaker's chop, as it was called. In the 1906 reform this dinner hour was abolished. The hour for meeting was then fixed at 2.45 instead of the previous 2.00. During the Second World War, black-out regulations made necessary further changes. The House then met at 11.00 a.m. and adjourned at 4.30, 5.30 or 6.30 according to the season of the year. After the war it was at first decided to meet at 2.15 and adjourn at 9.45. A year later this was changed to 2.30 and 10.30.

The first business of the House is question-time. Members may ask questions of ministers on matters relative to their official duties and every day's sitting except that on Friday begins with an hour's question-time. Questions are of two sorts, the starred and the unstarred.

If a star is attached to a question when it is handed in at the table, then an oral answer is requested. The relevant minister will attend in his place on the next day of his turn and if the question is reached—which is by no means certain if it comes low on the list—then he will rise at the Dispatch Box and give to it an oral answer. Ministers take turns to answer questions on a rota system. Since 1961 the Prime Minister has always answered at 3.15 on Tuesdays and Thursdays. Though it may be true that an adroit minister can always sidestep inconvenient questions and though the public may soon forget the revelations of the back-bencher's question (if it ever hears them), there is no doubt that the civil servants have a great dread of the P.Q.s, as they are called. The question is addressed to the minister: it contains no mention of any defaulting civil servant, but a civil servant who has been guilty of the blunder that is exposed is seriously alarmed that he will in the end suffer for it. The minister's answer may be followed, according to the Speaker's discretion, by a few supplementary questions, whether from the original questioner or from some other Member. If the question is unstarred, then it receives from the minister a written answer.

This device of question-time is something that foreign Parliaments do not have in exactly this form, and it is sometimes much belauded as evidence that there is much more effective control by the Legislature over the Executive here than elsewhere. In truth it is quite a desirable device but by no means of the overriding importance that is sometimes pretended. Some Members ask questions out of a genuine desire for information; some, usually of course Opposition Members, out of a bona fide ambition to criticise the minister. But there are Members whose main interest, it is always thought—particularly by fellow Members—is in their self-advertisement and to see their names on the order paper. It was discovered in 1970 that one third of all questions were asked by four per cent of the Members. The Lords too have a question-time, but it is more limited. Only four questions a day are permitted.

However, each question tends to have a rather longer run than a P.Q. in the Commons.

If he is not satisfied with the answer, the complaining Member in the Commons always has another opportunity: he can rise in his place and give notice that, owing to the unsatisfactory nature of the reply, he will 'raise the matter on the adjournment at the earliest opportunity'. He can then put his name down along with other Members who wish to raise their various grievances. Before long, if he persists, he will doubtless get the chance of an 'adjournment debate'. He then has the right, after the ordinary business of the House is finished, to hold a half-hour debate in which he raises his point and the minister or his under-secretary replies. But, again, these adjournment debates are unlikely to effect very much. There will probably not be anyone in the House except the Member who raises the question, the minister and perhaps a couple of Whips. There is, of course, no question of a division at the end. The hour is too late, the matter too unimportant for the national newspapers next morning to carry it. The only recompense for his trouble which the Member receives, if it so be that it is a matter for which this is a recompense, is that the local weekly paper in his constituency will probably carry an account of it, so that such constituents as are interested are made aware that their Member has raised the matter.

Before 1960 it was not permitted on the adjournment to refer to any request for new legislation. Now the Member who raises the debate may make 'incidental reference to a need for new legislation'. Members can also call attention to their grievances by putting down a motion and collecting in support of it the signatures of as many Members as may be agreeable. This motion will be put down on the order paper 'for an early day'. It is true that there is little or no chance of it being debated, but a formidable list of supporters may call the attention of the minister to a deep-seated grievance and have some effect. If the Government chooses to defy the motion, however, then, as was proved when a hundred Labour Members signed a motion against the placing of an airfield at Stansted, the initiative does not, in face of Government intransigence, usually prove very effective: when the Government challenged a debate, the Members voted in the lobby against their own motion.

After questions there follows any statement on public policy which a minister thinks it desirable to make. Parliament is jealous that first statements of new policies should be made in the House rather than on television or in the press. Then, after any ministerial statements, it is legitimate on two days of the week, if there be any Member who so wishes, that a back-bencher should seek to bring in a bill of his own choosing under what is called the Ten-Minute Rule: the Member introducing the bill can make a short speech and one Member can make a speech in opposition. The House then either gives leave to bring in the bill or, if it prefers, proceeds to a division. Unless the bill is thought by an overwhelming majority to be very offensive, leave to bring it in is usually given; but its chance of getting on to the Statute Book (that, is, becoming law) unless definitely favoured by the Government, is not very large, as these Ten-Minute-Rule bills rank for consideration below the bills of the private Members that are introduced by ballot. The device is generally valuable rather as a means of giving advertisement to an idea than with the hope of immediate legislative success.

After such business has been dealt with, the House then proceeds to the main business of the day. This goes on, unless the rule has been suspended, until 10 p.m. After that time there may be a prayer against some rules or instruments made by the Government under delegated legislation (see p. 133). Then follows the adjournment debate (see above). The House then rises to the cry of 'Who Goes Home?' from the attendants—a reminiscence of the day when Members required to be escorted back to their lodgings through the dangerous streets of London.

The main business of the day usually consists of a debate on a bill of one sort or another which the Government puts forward. The leading Members of the British Parliament are the ministers, who occupy its front bench. The general rules of procedure were settled in the seventeenth century when the House felt that its main business was to repel the Crown's encroachments on its freedom. Now it is the House's main business to support or to dismiss the ministers on its front bench. There has been over the years a steady growth in the proportion of Parliament's time devoted to Government business. Balfour, in what is known as his Parliamentary Railway Timetable in 1902, co-ordinated the machinery of the Executive's control over the Legislature. In the Standing Orders it is laid down that 'Wednesdays and Fridays before Easter and certain Fridays after Easter are reserved for private members, unless the House otherwise decides'. But in few years in recent times has the House (that is to say the Government) failed to decide otherwise, and during long periods— particularly during the wars—the private Member has entirely lost his right to introduce his own motions. In 1945 Attlee's Labour Government was particularly insistent on demanding for itself all the House's time. Its critics complained that this was because its socialistic programmes demanded the annexation to the State of powers and enterprises that had much better have been left in private hands. There was something in such a complaint. On the other hand the end of the war had left so much of the national life in need of reconstruction that, whatever Government had been in power, it would certainly have had to demand for itself wide powers to introduce sweeping reforms.

Parliament's part in legislation—though the House of Commons is often called the Legislature—is limited by the strength of party discipline which has grown up, as a result of which the greater number of divisions are straight party divisions. Members meekly obey their party Whip and vote as they are instructed to vote. Anyone who has any understanding of a Parliamentary system can see reason in the apparent paradox in this peculiar system. Equally, no one of sense can be blind to its dangers. It does no great harm for a man to vote with his party. It is very dangerous if he allows himself always to think and to speak with his party. Macaulay who was very much a party man, has written perceptively and pertinently on the danger of making too frequent party speeches. The debater's capacity to separate argument from belief was according to Macaulay 'the most serious of the evils which are to be set against the many blessings of popular government. The keenest and most vigorous minds of every generation, minds often admirably fitted for the investigation of truth, are habitually employed in producing arguments such as no man of sense would ever put into a treatise intended for publication—arguments which are just good enough to be used once when aided by fluent delivery and pointed language. The habit of discussing questions in this way necessarily reacts on the intellects of our ablest men, particularly of those who are introduced into Parliament at a very early age.'

The business of the day normally consists of a motion by a minister, its debate and at the conclusion its acceptance, either unanimously or as the result of a division. Much of the time is occupied by front-bench speakers—a first speech by the minister, a second speech from a front-bench Opposition speaker and at the end two winding-up speeches, one from the Opposition and the other from a Government front-bencher. In between, the back-benchers have to take such opportunities as come their way and in all important debates there are very many more anxious to speak than ever get called. Like the patients at the Pool of Bethesda, others get in before them. They have to go home at night with their speeches still undelivered in their pockets; and it is common enough for back-benchers, who have taken trouble to prepare their speech and imagine rightly or wrongly that they have something important to contribute, to be full of bile against what they regard as the unnecessary long-windedness and selfishness of the front-benchers. Such bile is impartially distributed between front-benchers on either side. Always in the House of Commons, side by side with the official battle between the two parties, is a secondary and unofficial battle of the back-benchers against the front benches. This unofficial battle showed itself most notably in the opposition to the scheme for the Reform of the House of Lords which had been arranged between the party leaders but which was most bitterly attacked and in the end defeated by both back benches; it came to a head in the complaints about the election of Mr. Lloyd to the Speakership.

Though in general debates are about a bill or an issue, it is sometimes desirable to have a debate on some subject (as, for instance, on foreign affairs) where a general discussion is more important than a division on a particular issue. Then the debate is held on some such motion as 'that this House take note of' such and such a document or 'that this House do now adjourn'. Adjournment motions are of various sorts. There is the half-hour adjournment motion after the business of the day has been completed. There is the emergency debate, when the Speaker allows the adjournment of the House to discuss some urgent matter of public importance. Or a motion for the adjournment may be a delaying tactic of the Opposition, or it may be a bona fide motion that the House should now adjourn and continue its discussion on a later day. Or it may be, as now, to make possible a wide debate unconfined by any particular rules of relevance: If there is no definite motion before the House, a speaker cannot be out of order. The usual Order of the Day is concerned with a debate and a decision either on the Government's motion or on some amendment to the motion. Members have a right to put down amendments to any motion. The amendment asks that certain words be omitted from or added to the existing motion. Members can put down as many amendments as they wish; it is for the Speaker to decide which of them shall be called. As a general rule, advance notice of an amendment is required, and it is then printed on the order paper, and Members are thus given an opportunity to study it. In exceptional circumstances the Speaker will sometimes accept a manuscript amendment.

The pressure of business on modern governments, of

whichever party, has compelled them to claim control of the Parliamentary programme to a far greater extent than was ever envisaged even by Balfour in 1902. The Government has its programme to get through and its first concern is to see that that programme is fulfilled. A session generally lasts about 160 sitting days. Of these 16 are at the disposal of private Members and 36 at the disposal of the Opposition. The rest are at the disposal of the Government. But such calculations are only estimates. It is always possible for the Government in the case of necessity to demand extra time. Equally, occasions arise when some great crisis makes it possible, or at least desirable, to surrender some time; but by and large the Government today pre-empts for its own business rather more than 100 days out of the 160 in every session. G. M. Young tells us in his *Essay on a Victorian Government* that in the last year of William IV's reign Parliament met on 88 days out of the 365. On seven days it was counted out—that is, there were insufficient Members present to make a quorum when a count was called. Twenty-eight days were days of Government business. The rest was private Members' time.

Though the Opposition has a right to choose the subject to be debated on Supply days (see p. 140), the Government can choose on what day those debates will be taken. The Government also has at its disposal a number of procedural devices, mostly first adopted to circumvent Parnell and still continued long after Parnell is dead and long after the Southern Irish have vanished from Westminster. There is the Closure—from the French word *Clôture*—by which a Member may move 'that the question be now put'. It is then for the Speaker to judge whether the matter has been sufficiently discussed. If he judges that it has, he accepts the motion. The House can then divide on it, but, if the motion has been moved by the Government Chief Whip, it is almost certain to be carried, though to be effective it is required that at least a hundred Members vote for it. If carried, the House proceeds to vote on the matter under debate. All Governments use the

closure from time to time. It was used 525 times between
1950 and 1970—that is on average about one day every
week that the House was sitting. The Speaker refused
during the same time 106 requests for it.

Secondly there is the guillotine. By the guillotine the
House, through the Government's exercise of its majority,
is compelled to accept a timetable for a bill by which so
much time shall be allowed for each section of it. At the
end of the allotted time the requisite portions and the
amendments on them are put to the House which must
accept or reject them without debate. Owing to the use of
this device, 111 of the 150 clauses in the Industrial Relations Bill of 1971 were never discussed at all. Until
recently a full day's debate had to be given to a guillotine
motion. Now it is possible to introduce it after a debate of
only three hours. The precise allocation of the time the
Government has decided to make available is decided by
a business committee, whose duty it is to see to it that the
time is distributed as reasonably as possible. Members of
both parties serve on that committee though, of course, the
Government Members have the majority and can in the
last resort carry the day if no generally acceptable arrangement can be reached. Sometimes it is possible to arrange a
timetable for bills by agreement 'through the usual
channels', without resort to compulsory procedure. This
was found possible on the Government of India Bill, 1935,
and on the Education Bill, 1944.

The guillotine is much less frequently employed than
the closure. It has been used since the war, on an average,
about once a year. It is unpopular with Members and
particularly if it is used on a matter upon which the
Government is receiving some opposition from Members
of its own party. For instance, Mr. Wilson did not dare to
employ it on the bill for the Reform of the House of Lords
in view of the vigorous all-party back-bench opposition to
it. This was a bill which was looked on as a battle between
the front and the back benches rather than as one between
the parties. Mr. Wilson would have earned great unpopularity with his own party if he had attempted to use

procedural devices to get it through and, meeting with opposition, preferred to abandon the bill. Mr. Heath, however, used this device in the European Communities Bill.

In general, the machinery of Parliament, particularly as it has developed over recent years, has given overwhelming power to the Executive over the Legislature. It is common enough to hear complaints both from backbenchers and from critics in the general public to the effect that the private Member is not more than a rubber stamp. People quote the saying of the historian Lecky that most of the duties of a Member of Parliament could be better performed by a fairly intelligent poodle dog. Mr. Macmillan, in an unguarded moment, said that it would be more convenient to everybody if they had the division first and the debate afterwards, since the day was long past when speeches made in the debate had any effect on the division. There is a good deal in the argument. Even those who argue—quite plausibly—that strict party discipline and the dominance of the Executive are on the whole more good than bad can hardly deny that it is a fact. 'Parliament really has no control over the Executive. It is a pure fiction,' said Lloyd George. The danger of the system is, one might argue, that it so hampers the activities of a Member of Parliament that it is no longer worth the while for a man of ability to become one. And it is certainly true that Parliament is no longer able to recruit independent men of letters as it was in the last century. Yet though it may perhaps be open to question whether the level of Members is today higher or lower than in the past, it cannot be pretended that there is any difficulty in finding a sufficient number of candidates willing to serve. Whenever there is a vacancy in any constituency that offers the least prospect of success the queue of candidates is still enormous. And, though examples of Members who are compelled to vote the party line in spite of their convictions are considerable, the story of the defeat of the House of Lords Bill of 1969 shows that revolts and protests of back-benchers against their front benches are not always ineffective.

When a debate has reached its end it is for the House to take its decision. The Speaker announces the question before the House, and Members then shout 'Aye' or 'No'. If the question is unopposed there is no reply of 'No' and the question is declared carried. If it is opposed the Ayes shout 'Aye' and the Noes 'No'. The Speaker declares 'I think the Ayes have it,' and the Noes, if they wish to persist in their challenge, repeat their 'No'. The Speaker then says: 'The House will proceed to a division.' He appoints two tellers for the Ayes and two for the Noes. Bells ring to summon the Members from their various occupations to the chamber. Six minutes are allowed from the Speaker's announcement. Then the Members troop into one or other of the division lobbies that run along the two sides of the chamber, the Ayes to the right and the Noes to the left. They troop through the lobby and their names are taken by the clerks behind the desks at the exit from the lobbies. The tellers count their number out loud. The tellers then go into the chamber and, standing before the table, announce the figures, the two tellers of the victorious side standing on the right, the two defeated on the left. The Speaker announces 'So the Ayes have it' (or the Noes, as the case may be).

This parade very arguably gives dignity to a single great division on the Second Reading (see p. 128), of an important bill. It impresses Members and those who see it, with the importance of the occasion. But when, as sometimes happens, the Opposition for reasons of obstruction forces division after division on some committee points, it is hardly sensible. I remember an occasion in 1947 when some Members of the Conservative Opposition employed such tactics and reduced Speaker Clifton Brown to pleading to the House 'Do you want to kill your Speaker?' The machinery was perhaps reduced to its ultimate farce when in March 1971, the Opposition insisted on forcing 33 continuous divisions on matters on which no debate had been held in their fight against the Industrial Relations Bill. Would it not be possible to avoid this tedious and absurd waste of time? Would it not be possible to devise

an electronic system by which each Member could record
his vote in an instant? No one can pretend that these
marathon votes serve any purpose of advertising to the
general public a party's deep feelings. The public hardly
notices such antics and, where it does notice them, dis-
misses them with ridicule. The effect of them is not to
further the cause of one side or the other but to bring the
whole machinery of Parliament into contempt. If push-
button voting were introduced there would be certain
practical problems. There would be the problem of making sure that one Member did not impersonate another to
attempt to vote twice. In other Parliaments each Member
has his own desk and can easily be made to vote from there.
At Westminster Members do not have their own seats.
Nevertheless these practical problems, though real, would
not, with ingenuity, be insurmountable. And it is hard to
think that in a world where so much is changing there
would be much lost in the abandonment of the present
cumbersome methods of voting. If Members did as a rule
vote out of their own conscience and by their own real
decision it might be argued that the device of a lobby was a
real influence causing men to act with responsibility.
Since they do not do that anyway, it is hard to see what
purpose is served by preserving the machinery.

3

The House's Reporting

As the House of Commons was, to begin with, no more
than a committee of the full Parliament, no record of its
proceedings was originally taken. There was no regular
record of the House's procedure before Elizabeth's time;
and when the House was fighting against the Stuart kings
it was thought highly undesirable that the public, and by
consequence the King, should know too much about what
was going on there. Charles I was excluded from its

meetings and until today the monarch is still rigorously excluded from its debates. Even after Parliament had established its sovereignty, it was still jealous of the public knowing too much about its business, and visitors were only admitted to hear its debates by the grace of Members. Biggar, the Irish Member, once impishly 'spied strangers' when the Prince of Wales, afterwards Edward VII, was listening to a debate, and he had to be made to leave. Defoe warned Parliament of the risk, in its hour of victory, of making itself as dangerous an enemy of the people's liberty as the kings were in the past, and the Wilkes case (see p. 70) showed the possibility of such Parliamentary unpopularity.

In the eighteenth century the question of the publication of Parliamentary proceedings was solved in a typically English fashion. Publication was still formally forbidden, but it became increasingly common, as was proved by Doctor Johnson in the *Gentleman's Magazine* of 1777, to publish accounts unofficially. Of course there was no guarantee that these unofficial accounts were accurate and indeed, as everybody knows, Doctor Johnson frankly confessed that he saw to it that the Whig dogs did not get the better of it. With the nineteenth century, common sense at last triumphed. It was agreed that if Members were thought of as responsible to their constituents it was only reasonable that their doings and their votes should be made public. In 1834 adequate facilities for reporting were made available and in 1836 the division lists began to be officially published. The official daily report of debates is known as *Hansard* after a family of printers and publishers that in the nineteenth century were associated with it. But *Hansard*, though an official record, is still only produced by leave of the House, and on a number of occasions during both the Great Wars the House held secret sessions from which *Hansard* was excluded and of which no record was permitted. By all accounts the revelations there made were not very startling as the Government had not sufficient confidence that any real secrets would not leak out. *Hansard* contains a record of all speeches, answers to questions and division lists. *Hansards* are also published of debates in Standing Committees (see p. 109). *Hansard's* reporters sit in the gallery of the chamber and take down verbatim all speeches. Members may go up afterwards to the *Hansard* office and there correct the proofs of their speeches. Acoustics in the chamber are not very good and Members sometimes find very amusing misreporting. (Sir Alan Herbert in his *Independent Member* records how his attacks on taxes on knowledge were all reported as attacks on taxes on Norwich.) A Member may correct mistakes of reporting. He must on no account alter the substance of his speech. What he has said he has said.

Today the issue has been not whether Parliament should be reported but whether it should be televised. A free vote in October 1972 decided against the intrusion of television into the chamber. Some of the arguments with which that controversy was fought out are similar to the arguments that were used 150 years ago when its reporting in the press was at issue. Parliament, we have been told, would be vulgarised if it were portrayed before the whole world on a television screen. To that surely the answer is that the authority of Parliament depends upon its popularity. For better or worse we have moved on into an age when the television screen is the main medium to the public of its information, and Parliament, if it is to survive in strength, must come to terms with the fact. Already ministers have come to think that their statements in Parliament are of secondary importance. They make them, but what they say to a somewhat somnolent audience of some thirty Members matters little to them. Their main anxiety is to get to a television screen and there explain to the millions what it is that they are about. The interest in the Westminster debate is by no means what it was. The newspapers no longer give full or serious reports to what happens in Parliament. The popular papers hardly report such goings-on at all. The circulation of *Hansard* has fallen dramatically: The sales fell from 8,889 in 1945 to 2,170 in 1963. The Members who are known to the public are not known because of their activities in Parliament but because of their frequent appearances on television. The personal prestige of a Member of Parliament has certainly declined. Perhaps that was inevitable with the decay of an aristocratic society.

If the decision against televising Parliament should ultimately be reversed there will admittedly be practical problems. What should be televised? The public certainly would not tolerate the total hogging of one channel by a full report of Parliament. Who is to do the editing, and how? Where are the cameras to be placed, and can they be so placed as not intolerably to dominate the debate? Will not the public be shocked by what they see, at the small number attending the debates and the casual, sprawling attitude of Members on their benches, the sometimes flippant and uncouth interruptions? These are problems the solution to which must be very carefully considered. They are difficult problems but they are not insoluble.

IV

THE COMMITTEES

1

The Jowett Plan

In a simpler aristocratic, basically agricultural society it was possible—or was thought possible—to leave the decisions of policy to men who were untried amateurs. In modern society problems tend to be highly technical problems on which the untrained cannot possibly have an opinion. One way or another advice must be brought in and, if the decisions are still nominally to be the decisions of Parliament, Members must be content to a large extent to take their decisions as rubber stamps, often not fully understanding what it is for which they are voting. So the power of the Executive over the Legislature has increased. We sometimes still say that we have Parliamentary government, but what we have in fact is Cabinet government. The Executive proposes all the main measures. All that Parliament can do is to sustain or refuse them. The strength of party machines has also increased. In the complex of problems on most of which they cannot pretend to an opinion of their own Members are usually glad of a Whip's discipline which can tell them 'Which side is ours?' They would not know how to vote without it. The thought of

> *Six hundred dull M.P.s*
> *In close proximity*
> *All thinking for themselves, is what*
> *No man could view*
> *With equanimity.*

Revolts are of course not unknown. But, in general, Members accept the party discipline and on the whole are grateful for it. That is the way the system works and the only way in which the system as it is could work.

But it is natural enough that the question should sometimes be raised whether the system is a right system. Its sternest critic was a now-forgotten, pre-1914-war Independent Labour Member for West Bradford, F. W. Jowett. He denounced the whole Parliamentary system as a fraud and a charade and would have substituted a totally pervasive committee system. The whole House according to him, should be divided into committees, each committee responsible for one or another of the departments of government. The minister who had a bill to propose should first have to carry it through the relevant committee before it was laid before the full House. He thought that thus the real examination should be before the committee, members of which would be expert and informed on the particular subject. The assent of the full Parliament would be in most cases more of a formality. Jowett's scheme had a certain similarity to that which has now been adopted for the Church of England. The Church of England is a State Church and therefore nominally its affairs are under the control of Parliament. But what may have been reasonable at a time when all the Members belonged to the Church of England and when a Test Act ensured that they at least nominally practised their religion to some minimal extent, could no longer be expected in the changed Parliament of today: with Members of every and no faith, with Members from Wales and Northern Ireland where there is no State Church and from Scotland which has a different State Church, and with only a minority of Members at all interested in the details of ecclesiastical legislation. No one could advocate that such a Parliament should exercise a control over the details of the Church's life. Therefore the Church Assembly and the Synod have been given power to legislate for the Church of England subject to an overriding veto being left to Parliament—a veto which in fact is very rarely invoked and which, as was proved when it rejected the Revised Prayer Book in 1927, is found to be very ineffective when invoked. But the difficulties in the concession of this semi-legislative power to a number of powerful committees is obvious. Supposing that the different committees adopted different policies, it would be difficult for a government to pursue a single coherent policy or to prevent the decisions of one minister from conflicting with those of another.

Lloyd George in 1931 advocated a scheme which was very similar to that of Jowett. But Lloyd George in 1931 had only a handful of followers—mostly his own relatives —in the House of Commons and no prospect of power. He by no means followed such policies when he was himself in office. Men of lively minds often advocate bold plans when they are in no danger of being called on to implement them. The only occasion when the country has been under the rule of unco-ordinated committees on something after the Jowett plan was under the Major-Generals in the Commonwealth, and the government which they provided was probably the most unpopular and the least successful that this country has ever suffered.

So few Members of Parliament have the qualifications to discuss the details of industrial policy and industrial processes that suggestions have been often made that these discussions could more properly take place elsewhere than in the House of Commons. Of course they very often do take place—profitably or unprofitably—in a hundred other places, in committees and meetings of consultation all through the land but these meetings have no constitutional status. There have been at times some suggestions that it would be a good plan to establish some sort of Parliament of Industry. Sydney Webb made such a suggestion in his *Constitution for a Socialist Commonwealth of Great Britain*. Winston Churchill in his Romanes lecture of 1930 put forward a similar demand for a House of Industry. So did Leo Amery in his *Thoughts on the Constitution*. But though the project was for some time in the air it never attracted attention and is little heard of today. If it was to be seriously considered, very detailed work would obviously have to be done to settle what exactly were to be the features and powers of this House of Industry.

2

Committees of the Whole House

To the justifiable complaint that Parliament's tray is overloaded—and with matter so highly technical that six hundred Members cannot be expected to pay proper attention to its details—the most fashionable reply is that we should develop the committee system (though not indeed on quite the scale Jowett envisaged).

There are three sorts of committees known to Westminster, radically different from one another: the standing committee, the select committee and the party committee. If a bill passes its Second Reading (see p. 128), it has to go on to a committee stage where its details will be considered clause by clause, amendments discussed and, if passed, inserted into the revised text. There are two sorts of committees on bills—committees of the Whole House and standing committees. A Committee of the Whole House means the House of Commons meeting in a slightly different and less formal manner from its normal debates. Instead of the Speaker presiding over it in his robes from his chair, one of the chairmen of committees or deputy speakers presides. These committees of the Whole House date from the early part of the seventeenth century. The House at that time often did not have full confidence in the Speaker. He was thought (at least before Speaker Lenthall) to be the creature of the King rather than of Parliament; and therefore, to prevent any danger that he would hand-pick a special committee of the King's friends who might water down some measures unwelcome to the King, the House dissolved itself in its formal persona and met instead as a committee to be presided over not by the Speaker but by an officer of its own—in whose appointment the King had no say—the Chairman of Committees.

At a later date, when menace from the Speaker was no longer feared, it was decided that the Chairman of Committees might act in need as the Speaker's deputy and preside over a full session of the House from the Speaker's chair. The Committee of the Whole House is a meeting at which any Member can speak or vote. It is like a full meeting of the House in everything except a few technical details. Debate is freer and somewhat less formal than in the full House. If the Bill is at all a technical bill upon which only experts have a useful opinion, it is often a very tedious business. 'One of the most hopeless exhibitions of helpless ingenuity and wasted mind,' said Bagehot, 'is a Committee of the Whole House on a bill of many clauses which eager enemies are trying to spoil and various friends are trying to mend.'

Its debates indeed even to this day are often very fatuous affairs. In the box behind the Speaker sit the civil servants who are to prompt the minister. He has to turn to them if any novel difficulties arise, but both he and they have already come to the chamber having agreed what concessions, if any, are to be made, and concessions are made or refused quite irrespective of who has had the better of the exchanges of debate. Speeches are made, the division bells ring and the back-benchers troop in to support their minister in the lobby, quite ignorant probably of what has been the subject under debate.

The important so-called Acts of Parliament are then in reality acts proposed by the Cabinet to Parliament and more or less imposed on it. A sensible Government of course takes steps to see that its acts are popularly acceptable and therefore consults relevant bodies of public opinion—employers, trade unionists and the like—before it brings in its bills. Pressure groups thus have plenty of opportunities to exercise their influence—too much opportunity, some say—and public opinion can express itself. But that influence is brought to bear before the bill is introduced. Even the back-bench Member, in so far as he can exercise influence, is much more likely to do so in a party committee upstairs before the bill is introduced than by a speech on Second Reading or by an amendment on the floor of the House. By the time that the bill is introduced, the Government has committed itself and it is very difficult to get it to change. Cabinets with rare exceptions are able to carry through Parliament whatever measures they propose. Three times since the war in 1950, 1951 and 1965 a Government has had a very narrow majority but that has not led to its defeat on the floor of the House. It has been able to pass its legislation, though the legislation has been less adventurous than it would have been had the majority been larger. The only year that recorded singular failure of the Government in its legislation was 1969, when Mr. Wilson's Government abandoned its plan for the reform of the House of Lords in face of attacks from back-benchers. It abandoned its bill for constituency boundary revision when it was rejected by the Lords; and the bill, promised in the Queen's speech, for a revision of industrial relations was, in face of criticism from the trade unions outside the House and from left-wing Labour Members inside it, never brought in. But by and large the Cabinet rules. When it has to modify its policies it does so not because of the criticism of Parliament but because of the force of events.

3

Parliament and Nationalised Industries

In earlier centuries the State believed in a considerable amount of *dirigisme* of the individual's economic activity, but the principle of the nineteenth century was a principle of laissez-faire. Industrialism grew up therefore under a philosophy which did not believe in national ownership, though for some strange reason neither Britain nor any other country has ever used a private postal service (it is not very clear why). But, with that exception, there was little nationalised industry in the nineteenth century, and, until 1945, only a handful of experiments in public ownership, such as the B.B.C., London Transport and British Airways. In 1945, however, the Labour Party came into power committed to the national ownership of what is called the high peaks of the economy, and the Parliament of 1945 carried through extensive measures of nationalisation. One of the major modern Parliamentary problems has been to find the exact manner of organising these nationalised industries.

The word 'nationalisation' had been bandied about in political debates ever since the Labour party, twenty-five years before, had become one of the main parties of the state. By most of those who used it, it was assumed that the Labour plan was to take over the industries and manage them as Government departments in much the same way in which the Post Office was then managed. Sir Stafford Cripps and other Socialist writers had terrified us with fearful threats of a total suppression of Parliamentary liberty in order to carry through the Socialist policy. Happily these threats were not fulfilled—indeed by the time that the Socialists came into office they were quite forgotten. On the other hand, when they came into office and clamoured for nationalisation the quite extraordinary discovery was made that almost no thought had been given to what they meant by nationalisation—to how the nationalised industries were to be managed. According to the plans that were eventually adopted, it was decided that these industries should not be put under the direct control of a minister subject to questioning in Parliament but under Government-appointed boards whose day-to-day administration was to be free from Parliamentary question. What has been established is more nearly what Mr. Burnham in his book of that name would call a managerial society than a Socialist society. In what way it was ever intended by the Socialists that Government or public authority would have any control of these industries was far from clear. The Executive has a certain control at any rate in the sense that ministers could, and from time to time did, dismiss their chairmen, but Parliament's control was very small. According to the constituting acts, the nationalised industries were under obligation to pay their way. But they did not in fact do so and, if they did not, there was nothing that Parliament could do except accept the fact of their deficit. The problem was by no means solved in the constituting acts nor has it ever been solved since. A Select Committee on Nationalised Industries has been set up by which Members, or those of them who are specially interested, endeavour to keep an eye on how the industries are managed. The consequences of the wide expansion of public or semi-public authority has been the establishment of a number of authorities whose exact relation of subordination to central authority is often far from clear. Like the Prices and Incomes Board they come and go with the changing whims of changing ministers. Roads, electricity, broadcasting— these matters have been sometimes managed well and sometimes managed ill. Often opinions differ whether they have been managed well or ill. They certainly have not been managed on any single coherent plan.

The nationalising acts require the minister to appoint a Chairman and Board of Management. The Board is—at any rate according to the Act, whatever may happen in practice—under obligation to balance its accounts over a period. The minister had certain broad powers, such as that of making safety regulations, but the day-to-day management of the industry is the responsibility of the Board. Idealistic Socialists who imagined that the workers would be inspired by a new enthusiasm at the thought that they were working for the community rather than, as previously, for private profit-seekers have been much disappointed. Relations in nationalised industries have generally been more disturbed than in those of private ownership. Parliament has the right to an annual debate on any nationalised industry, and has also from time to time further opportunities for discussing it, if it asks for increased borrowing powers or the like; but under the eagle eye of the Whips, Parliament's power of control does not amount to much. There is a strict control of the questions which the private Member can ask of the minister at question-time. A rather wider latitude is permitted on the matters which he is allowed to raise in an adjournment debate.

4

Standing Committees

In the seventeenth century it was difficult to get Members to attend Parliament. As we have said, in the division on the Grand Remonstrance, for instance, only 307 Members out of the total House of 580 voted. So the habit grew of getting promises to attend from a small number of Members who would agree to serve on a standing committee. At first the King selected the members of these standing committees; he selected people on whom he thought that he could rely. It was a mark of what Notestein calls 'the winning of the initiative' when towards the close of the century the House won the right to choose its own committees. Until 1907 committee stages of all public bills were in a Committee of the Whole House unless it was ordered otherwise. In 1907 the rule was reversed and the normal plan was now to send most bills to a standing committee of probably about thirty Members selected in strict proportion to party strength in the House, and only bills considered to be of major constitutional importance were by a special vote henceforth to be considered by a Committee of the Whole House. There are normally about six of these standing committees between which the bills that are at any moment in passage through the House are distributed.

In committee the bill is considered clause by clause, amendments to each clause proposed and, if desired, passed. The bill in its amended form is then reported back to the House which, on Report Stage, considers whether it wishes to accept the bill in this new form, and has the opportunity of making further amendments. Then follows the Third Reading at which only formal verbal amendments can be considered.

The debate in a standing committee follows the forms of the House. Members rise when they wish to speak and wait for the chairman to call them. They address one another as 'Honourable Members'. But the Members on the two sides, instead of having a gangway between them, are divided only by a desk and the debate is even more relaxed than in a Committee of the Whole House. Decisions are taken by a roll-call and voting is on much less rigid party lines than in the chamber. With the complexities of amendments it is often difficult for a Member to know whether he should say 'Aye' or 'No'. I remember a famous occasion when a chairman said, 'All those in favour say "No".' A harmless but not very bright under-secretary said timidly 'No' and the chairman then answered 'The Ayes have it.'

There are, then, these standing committees which in the modern press of legislation are increasingly used by Government. Their authority is limited, for any amendments which they make have to be reported back to the full House which can reject them on Report if it so wishes. The committees generally meet on Tuesdays and Thursdays in the morning and finish by lunch-time. Thus it is hoped that Members will be free to attend in the full chamber in the afternoon. But on occasion of especial difficulty the minister in charge compels them to meet also at other and less convenient times. When that happens there are always loud complaints from Opposition Members.

5
Select Committees

Quite apart from the standing committees are the select committees. These committees have developed considerably in recent years as the answer to the demand that the back-bench Member should be given more responsible work to do, and are largely inspired by the model of other countries—particularly of America and France. Committees should be established, we are told, detailed to the various departments of state. A Member should join the committee on the subject in which he is interested. He would then be able to make himself expert on this subject. His committee would have the right to summon witnesses and to receive confidential information and could, it is alleged, keep a much more valuable control on the minister than was possible from criticisms of the general member with no especial source of information.

There are some, like Mr. Michael Foot, who value highly debates in full Parliament on the floor of the House and who would reject any attempts to make small committees the true forum of criticism of ministers. There is something to be said for their point of view. Nevertheless, there is a general opinion among Parliamentarians that greater use should be made of the committee system in some form or other and that the final debates in the House would be enriched rather than impoverished if the Government's critics had better facilities to equip themselves with the facts. Whatever the defects of the committee system, Professor Anthony Barker and Professor Michael Rush discovered from investigation for their *M.P. and his Information* that 73 per cent both of Tory and Labour Members approved of them. There is little prospect of them totally changing the nature of British Parliamentary processes to the satisfaction of Jowett's ambition. But there is a general feeling that they are on the whole worth supporting and encouraging. It is sometimes objected, for instance by Mr. Henry Fairlie, that if the committees were constituted in proportion to party strengths, as they are, their votes would be as automatic as those on the floor of the House. But this is not true even today of standing committees, still less of select committees. Nor would it be the main purpose of these committees to vote on party issues. Their main purpose would be to elicit information. Some think that there should be a duplication of committees—one to assist in the formulation of policy and another to conduct an audit on how legislation is working. The wisdom of this is doubtful.

There is no reason to think that we have not lessons to learn from the American practice. Yet it is important to decide exactly what lessons. First, are all the American committees as powerful and effective as is sometimes thought? Are not many of the generalisations derived from the experience of the Fulbright Committee and very little else? It is true that Senator Fulbright's committee on foreign relations has attracted to itself very great attention and has beyond question played an important part in shaping public opinion and in uncovering information which it has been able to pass on to the public. But it is concerned with a subject—foreign affairs—in which, in this disturbed state of the world, the public is intensely interested. Senator Fulbright has given it outstanding leadership. The Ways and Means Committee is also powerful and important. But there are many other committees on subjects of less general interest of which we hear less and which have less effect. Secondly—and from this point of view more important—there is of course the total difference between American and British constitutional practice. The American minister does not sit in Congress. The American congressman, even if he is of the President's party, is under no obligation to support the Administration on every vote. No minister has to resign if a vote is given against him. There is no question-time in

Congress. A minister can give a press conference if he wishes, but if he does not wish, no one can compel him. The Congressional committees are the only places where he can be compelled to explain and defend his policy. The British system is, as we know, entirely different.

Ministers will always remain primarily answerable to the House as a whole. Nevertheless a number of select committees have usefully cross-examined ministers in the course of their inquiries. Although the composition of select committees reflects party strength in the House, they do not as a rule in practice work on partisan lines and Government Members may be just as assiduous in uncovering 'skeletons' or probing weaknesses in administration as Opposition Members. When it comes to drafting the report, straight party voting in select committees is rare.

The Parliamentary parties maintain an element of control over select committees since the names of those who serve on the different committees emerge through 'the usual channels' (i.e. the Whips' offices). It is not unknown for a Member to be kept off a committee on which he wishes to serve, or to be dropped from a committee, as a punishment. Successive governments rather than the House itself have the final say in the work of select committees by determining what their terms of reference shall be.

In all the suggestions for such committees that have been made the Government has always insisted that it keeps in its own hands the power to remove any chairman whom it thinks obstreperous, a very different situation from that which Senator Fulbright enjoys. When the Select Committee on Nationalised Industries was established, it was invited to investigate any policies or practices in such industries 'except where the policies had been decided by, or clearly engaged the responsibility of, any minister'. It was a considerable reservation; the British system being what it is, perhaps an almost inevitable one. If we are to preserve the British system at all, the fundamental decisions on policy must be the responsibility of

the Cabinet and the effective vote on them not the vote of
an expert committee but of Parliament as a whole. In fact
the only condition of enlarged freedom is that the Government should consent to do less altogether, that a smaller
area of our life should come under the control of public
authority at all, that we should be allowed to decide more
for ourselves. Is there any chance of this happening? It is
easy to make rounded demands that the people should be
left free. How likely is it in fact that the Government will
abandon controls which it has once seized? It is easy to
demand that the number of civil servants should be reduced. The victory usually goes in practice to Parkinson's
Law, and civil servants breed more civil servants.

There are at present ten sessional committees, four
appointed in pursuance of standing orders: the Committee
on Public Accounts, on the Standing Committees, the
Committee of Selection, and an Expenditure Committee
which in 1970 was substituted for the previous Estimates
Committee. Six committees are appointed by sessional
order: the Committee of Privileges, the Committee of
Public Petitions, the Select Committee on Statutory
Instruments, the Select Committee on Nationalised Industries, the Select Committee of the House of Commons
(Services) and the Select Committee on the Parliamentary
Commissioner. There are also departmental committees
on the work of particular departments: on agriculture,
education and overseas aid. Unlike the standing committees, they can form their own procedure. The Select
Committee on Science and Technology is one that has
firmly established a regular existence. Some select committees are 'one-off jobs' set up to investigate a specific
non-recurrent matter, such as the committee which
reported in July 1972 on the 'planting' of Parliamentary
questions.

Those who approve of the committees do not on the
whole want them to change policy. They want to be informed of policy. They want to be in the know, or at least
feel that they are in the know. Shortly after Mr. Heath
came into power in the summer of 1970 Mr. William

Whitelaw issued a Green Paper in which he gave the new Government's support for the continuance, though not the extension, of the committee system. He approved of what had been done, but did not wish to increase committee membership for fear that there would not then be a sufficiency of Members to take part in the debates on the floor of the House.

His critic might reply that a developed committee system would not detract from the debate on the floor of the House but enhance it by increasing the chance that the Government's critics would be properly informed. The Select Committee on Procedure has suggested the formation of a Committee on Taxation and Economic Affairs. But the Treasury reports that it is unlikely that the Government would 'advise' the House to form such a committee. The true reason for the Government's hesitancy about a Select Committee on Economic Affairs, think Mr. Peter Jay and Mr. Samuel Brittan, in their *Case for a Select Committee on Economic Affairs*, 'are, we believe, the same as those which have tempted all governments in all countries at all times to minimise the amount of explaining which they have to do—the fear of giving hostages to fortune.' 'I am myself,' said Mr. Whitelaw, 'strongly of the opinion that the place for political controversy is the chamber, and that a select committee cannot be successful if the matters which it is considering are so charged with controversy that its members align themselves on party lines.' The committee, say the Treasury in their written evidence, might stray too far into 'policy formulation'. The floor of the House is the place for debate and 'in the British context the natural course is for Members through questions and in the course of debate or in some other way to ask the responsible minister what proposals he has'— with the Whips to see that these proposals are accepted whether the answers are satisfactory or not.

An unsolved problem for these committees is the problem of staffing. The Nationalised Industries Committee in its early days called for qualified expert staff to help in its investigations, but this was not provided. The Select

Committee on Science and Technology, first appointed in December 1966, gave itself to a study of the nuclear research programme. When it was half-way through, the Government asked it to examine the entirely different subject of the *Torrey Canyon* disaster. The Committee has since turned to other major fields such as defence research and population policy. In its reports the committee has commented on the wholly inadequate staff with which it was asked to do its work. Its accusation was that the House had agreed to an extension of the committee system without any consideration of the staff required if the new committees were to perform their functions properly.

By present arrangements, the Public Accounts Committee, whose duty it is to examine public expenditure only after the money has been spent, and which has sat since 1861, is to be maintained. But by its side the Estimates Committee has been expanded into a Select Committee on Expenditure which is concerned with the programme of future spending, and the policies that the estimates of expenditure imply. Whether it will be possible for this Committee and its sub-committees, each of which specialises in a particular area of government activity, to do any effective work without infringing on the Cabinet's right to decide policy remains to be seen. At the same time Mr. Heath has established a 'central capability unit' to review Cabinet policy. Again it remains to be seen whether this form of duplicating decisions and setting up one body to watch another will be successful. Mr. Wilson's attempt to set up Mr. George Brown's Department of Economic Affairs to work alongside, and sometimes against, the Treasury was not altogether successful —whether because of personal difficulties or because of the inherent impossibility of asking two men to take decisions that must of their nature be single decisions, who shall say?

It is a commonly-heard mutter among the back-benchers that the real battle at Westminster is not between the parties but a battle of the front-benchers against the back-benchers. There is a degree of truth in this suspicion. The front-bench holder of an office, or a member of the Opposition with the experience of office in the past and prospects of regaining it in the future, with his prescriptive right to be called in debate whenever he rises in his place, has much less reason to feel frustration than the back-bencher, and therefore arrangements which seem intensely irritating to the back-bencher will often appear convenient and reasonable enough to the Privy Councillor. Though it is not wise publicly to confess as much, there are in fact many front-bench politicians and civil servants who think that modern industrial society can only work if it is worked as a totalitarian unity. Eccentricity and independence of conduct can no longer be tolerated.

The object of any reforms that might be introduced would, in their view, be not to give to the back-bencher any real increase of influence over policy but the reverse: to concede to him as little as possible, and to make sure that any concessions were concessions of window-dressing that amounted to nothing effective. At present the back-bench critic's attempt to expose the minister is, as we have said, not often effective because the battle is so unequal. The minister has all the machinery of the Civil Service behind him to provide him with information. The critic's powers to equip himself with information are very meagre. It is often argued that the British M.P. is both worse paid and equipped with scantier facilities than any in other industrial nation. He ought, it is said, to be provided with more research assistance and better facilities. There is much force in such contentions but the arguments about them all oscillate in a vacuum because whatever lip-service may be paid, the front-benchers have by no means as yet made up their minds whether they really want the back-bencher to have more effective powers of criticism. Do they really think it is desirable that back-benchers should be given more power? Or do they rather think that we have moved into a closely interlocked society where all real power must be kept in the hands of the Executive, if the system is to work at all? And are concessions to back-benchers really intended to work, or is it rather a question of inventing devices which might give them an appearance of authority so as to keep them quiet? 'Don't waste too much time on the party committee,' was, according to Mr. Julian Critchley in *The Times* of February 20, 1971, Mr. Macmillan's advice to a new Member. 'They were invented by the Whips after the 1931 elections to keep our majority out of mischief.' Indeed many of the back-benchers themselves are not quite certain how sincere they are in their demands. How often have we seen a young Member come up to Westminster bursting with plans by which, as he claims, the mumbo jumbo of Parliament will be washed away and reality substituted for the façade? In two or three years' time all too often the greater part of his enthusiasm will have evaporated. Whether this is because he has come to see that there is more sense in some of the ancient antics of Westminster than was at first apparent, or merely because he has discovered that changing things is enormously difficult and, his energy abated, he prefers to sit back and go along with the system; or because he has discovered that if he continually makes a nuisance of himself, promotion and favour are unlikely to come his way, who can say? Each case has its own history.

As anyone who has sat for some years in Parliament must have noticed, the life there has an almost inevitable effect on the character. Power corrupts but absence of power corrupts absolutely and the absence of the possibility of power even more than anything else. The peculiar danger of the politicians, if we except a very few persons in supreme positions, is not that they are very powerful but that custom compels them in their public speeches to be continually pretending to be more powerful than they really are. The disciplines of the party system also have their effect on the character. Party organisation demands that in all but the most unimportant questions the individual is content to toe the party line, and if he supports the party line with his vote it is at least convenient for him to support it in his speeches whether inside or outside the House. The alternative of explaining the exact subtlety of his position is exhausting. The easy temptation into which many Members fall is to cease thinking for themselves and merely to repeat the convenient party patter.

Perhaps the greatest virtue of the select committees is that their tradition is to conduct their investigations on other than party lines. They do not get very much publicity and it will be for the benefit of the characters of the Members to live a larger part of their life away from publicity. It is good for the soul of a politician to serve on a select committee. On the other hand if the select committees should get very important they then would become corrupted by publicity.

Select committees are generally committees solely of the House of Commons. Occasionally joint committees of both Houses are established. The one to consider the revision of theatre censorship was a case in point.

My friend Mr. Henry Fairlie in his *The Life of Politics* has very truly said that I was not 'an effective Member'. No Member who went to Parliament can ever have effected less. It would be too much like an exercise in sour grapes to say that I never wanted to have success, but I think I can fairly say that I never wanted it so intensely— success never suggested itself to me as a supreme good— and the competition is so intense that those who do not want it utterly and without qualification have little hope of getting to the top. I would have accepted success if they had offered it to me on a plate, but success in politics does not come thus.

6

Party Committees

There is also a third set of committees: the unofficial party committees of the two parties, both the general party committee of the Parliamentary Labour party and the 1922 Committee of the Conservative party, and the particular committees which try to keep an eye on the various departments of policy—Foreign Affairs, Defence, Education, Health and the like. These meet in the various committee rooms upstairs, and have no official standing in the constitution. They debate, and perhaps decide what attitude the party will take in matters that are about to come up in the House. It is natural that persons engaged on a common purpose should meet together to co-ordinate their policies. Such meetings must always have taken place at every date and in every form of society. The present only differs from past ages in that the meetings are more formalised. In past, more amply servanted, ages politicians tended to get together in comfortable private houses or in West-End clubs (the Conservatives predominantly at the Carlton Club). Most Labour Members have not got West-End clubs and few of them have large country houses. Therefore these meetings tend to take place in the House's committee rooms to a much greater extent than in the earlier times. These party meetings are all in theory confidential, but enterprising journalists usually find some way of discovering what has happened at them—or at any rate what they allege to have happened. These disclosures, or pretended disclosures, are often resented by Members and immediately after the Second World War one Labour Member was very severely punished for having sold the secrets of his party meetings to the press.

V

LEGISLATION, DIRECT

AND DELEGATED

It is common enough to speak of Parliament as the Legislature. If we go back to the Middle Ages, we find a time when Parliament passed its resolutions but the King transformed them into actual statutes. A little later, and indeed right up to the Civil War, Parliament was really a legislature. The King was the head of the Executive. Parliament, by its legislation, laid down the rules within which he could execute—in particular the taxes that he could levy. In Henry VIII's time Parliament passed a Statute of Proclamation enabling the King to make laws as he saw fit. But that was a unique concession made to no other sovereign. In general, political life was one of attempted balance between the Sovereign and Parliament. Sometimes the balance was achieved. Sometimes it failed of achievement. Even after the Civil War and the revolution of 1688 when the minister, still nominally the King's minister as indeed he still is, was in reality dependent on a Parliamentary majority and subject to dismissal by Parliament, Parliament still remained the Legislature in the sense that the greater number of laws passed were private bills, brought in by private members, granting privileges to private citizens—for an enclosure of land, for instance, in the eighteenth century, or for the building of railways in the nineteenth. The eighteenth century, though a century of Parliamentary sovereignty, was a century very barren of constitutional legislation. With the reform of Parliament after the Acts of 1832 and 1867, with the growth of industrialism and the beginnings of social reforms the volume of direct Government legislation began to increase and in recent years has increased very much more rapidly.

Today Parliament is still theoretically the Legislature in the sense that no measure can become the law unless it has, directly or indirectly through the action of some body to whom Parliament has delegated authority, been passed by Parliament. Every such measure has to be passed by the House of Commons and by the House of Lords, or has to be passed twice by the Commons against the Lords' veto in accordance with the Parliament Acts, and to receive the royal assent before it becomes law. A law is 'enacted by the Queen's Most excellent Majesty, by and with the consent of the Lords Spiritual and Temporal and Commons in this Parliament assembled'. But in fact in modern times the great majority of laws are proposed by the ministers to Parliament and to a large extent are automatically voted by the Government's supporters in the House, often with very imperfect understanding of what it is that they are voting about. The Opposition, of course, is equally un-informed as it votes against the measure proposed. In fact, as has been said, the Government that we have today is not Parliamentary Government but Cabinet Government, and the main business of the Leader of the House and of the Whips is to plan a timetable in accordance with which the Government can get its legislative programme through Parliament, and the test of their success is measured by the extent to which they are able to get that programme implemented.

1

Private Members' Bills

In theory any Member of Parliament can introduce a bill and, of course, back-bench Members still have a number of opportunities to propose legislation: through bills proposed by those who have been successful in the ballot; through bills introduced under the Ten-Minute Rule; and indeed at other times any Member may give notice of his intention to introduce a bill. There are thus still facilities for a private Member to introduce a bill: his chances of getting it on to the Statute Book (passed into law) are another matter. An order passed by the Commons in each session specifies the number of days that are to be reserved for private Members' bills. At present the number is sixteen—sixteen Fridays. A ballot is held and as a result of this ballot about twenty-five Members are successful and acquire the right to bring in a bill on any subject of their choice, provided that it does not impose a charge on the taxpayer. A Member who is successful in the ballot but not successful in drawing the first place for one of the reserved Fridays can hang around on his appointed afternoon in the hope that the bill before his will suddenly collapse and thus give him the chance to bring in his bill. But if the other bill should run on, he does not get his chance. Even the prospects of the Member who draws a place entitling him to the first debate of the day are not very favourable. He is not likely to have the facilities for consultation with outside interests that would be open to a minister bringing in a Government bill. He will have to draft the bill without the assistance of the expert Parliamentary draftsmen, and it is likely that without such assistance the bill on its original presentation will contain drafting difficulties that will make it easily vulnerable. This may lead, or help to lead, to its defeat on Second Reading and, if it fails there, that is of course the end of it. But, if it passes Second Reading, that by no means gives assurance that it will by the end of the session get on to the Statute Book. It still has to get through its committee stage and, if it has vigorous opponents, opportunities for delay in committee are numerous. By and large a controversial bill has little chance of getting through all its necessary stages to the Statute Book unless there is such evidence of its general popularity that the Government decides to assist its progress, perhaps by giving it more time or by putting at its disposal the services of the Parliamentary draftsmen so as to free it from incidental verbal confusion.

All the important acts of the late nineteenth and the earlier twentieth centuries have been Government acts, and in the 1930s it was common enough to say that a private Member's bill had no hope of getting on to the Statute Book unless it was on a matter so trivial as to arouse no controversy at all. The only point, it was said, if indeed there was a point, in bringing in such bills, was to advertise one's cause. A number of modern examples— bills on abortion, for the reform of the homosexual laws, for the regulation of obscene publications—have shown that generalisation to be too sweeping. The machinery of the private Member's bill has been found convenient for the promotion of the so-called 'permissive society'—for measures which Home Secretaries favour in their private capacity but which the Government is unwilling publicly to include in its programme for fear of electoral odium.

The first and perhaps the most notable of these successful enterprises of the private Member was A. P. Herbert's divorce bill. Until recently the Churches—in particular the Church of England and the Church of Rome—still demanded that the secular law should be obedient to what they interpreted as the law of God, and by consequence opposed all proposals for easier divorce. On the other hand society had by now become largely secularised and there were many who thought that the Churches might, if they wished, impose their discipline on their own members but that it was no longer tolerable that they should impose it by the secular code on those who were not of their flock. Nevertheless it was all too probable that any proposal for easier divorce would arouse strong clerical hostility, and many who might privately favour it were not willing to champion it in public.

In the election of 1935 A. P. Herbert—rather to most people's, and indeed, as he confessed, to his own surprise —was returned as one of the burgesses for Oxford University. He had stood as an Independent and had circulated to his electors an election address of unprecedented length, in which he enumerated all the causes which, if elected, he would promise to support and champion. Most prominent among these causes was the reform of the divorce laws. Therefore, when successful, he felt himself under obligation to redeem this promise. Betting, as he confesses, in his book *Independent Member*, was very strong among Members of Parliament against his meeting with any success. Michael Beaumont, a friendly opponent, said that odds as high as a thousand to one would have been laid against him.

At the beginning of every Parliament a book is set out on a certain day in one of the division lobbies. In that book all Members who wish to bring in a private Member's bill are invited to write their names against a certain number. The Clerk of the House then draws out and reads out the successful numbers and the Speaker announces the name of the Member to whom one of the numbers corresponds. Such Members have then the right to introduce whatever bill they see fit. A. P. Herbert naturally went and wrote his name down in this book and, if his lucky number had turned up, he would have surmounted the first hurdle of his race. Mr. David Steel did receive this good fortune to his plans for introducing the Termination of Pregnancies Bill—his bill for regularising the abortion law—which has got to the Statute Book in recent years. But A. P. Herbert had no such good fortune. Therefore his only chance of getting his bill introduced was to find some Member who had had the luck of the draw and who had no bill of his own to hand and would be willing to sponsor it. Time was very limited, as Members had to announce the bill that they were proposing to bring in that same afternoon. Herbert's task was no easy one. Several Members, when approached, were unwilling either because they had causes of their own or because they thought divorce too hot to hold and likely to bring them into trouble with their constituents. However he was in the end successful. Rupert de la Bère, himself, like Herbert, a new Member and whom Herbert had until then not known even by sight, agreed to introduce the bill. De la Bère had won the second place in the ballot and the Whips had furnished him with an innocuous bill about Municipal Elections which they suggested that he should present. De la Bère had, as he confessed, up till then had no special interest in the divorce problem but he consented to drop the Municipal Elections bill and take up Herbert's measure. Therefore when the day for the bill's Second Reading came, De la Bère moved it. Herbert and others spoke in its favour and, rather to the general surprise, on the division it was supported by 78 votes to 12. The vote on the Second Reading of a private Member's bill is almost always small because on every other day Members are kept compulsorily in the House by the command of their Whips. Private Members' Friday is the only unwhipped day. So Members naturally take advantage of it to get down to their constituencies or to begin their week-end holidays. It is often one of the main problems of the mover of a private Member's bill to keep at Westminster a sufficient number to form a quorum and thus prevent the House from being counted out. In any event, the vote on this bill showed that, while the number that was keen on divorce law reform might be small, the number opposed to it was nugatory.

The bill, having passed its Second Reading, had next, like any other bill, to go to its standing committee upstairs. There is a special standing committee which deals with all private Members' bills. Government bills are steered through their standing committee by the relevant minister. With a private bill Herbert had of course himself to manage the committee stage. But, as often happens, the House, having shown its general desire to have the bill, the Government considered it their duty to give it fair play. The National Government was then in power, and although, as Herbert records, at least two of the Government Whips were personally opposed to the bill, yet they made sure that it was not destroyed on some technicality. Sir Thomas Barnet, the Treasury Solicitor, helped Herbert in drafting problems. One of the Law Officers sat throughout the committee debates beside him and helped with technical advice. The bill always had the advantage that there were more Members in favour of it than against it, and therefore its points were always likely to be carried on a challenge. Herbert's main difficulties, as is apt to happen in Parliamentary business, was on incidentals. The opening of the committee happened to coincide with Edward VIII's abdication crisis. This created an atmosphere in which no one was anxious to spend his time sitting in a committee on a private Member's bill and Herbert's main difficulty was in ensuring the attendance of a sufficient quorum to save the meeting from being adjourned.

Eventually the bill got through its committee stage and was ready for report and Third Reading before the full House. There the problem was that of time. The bill had to be on the Statute Book before the end of the session or it lapsed. They lost one of the private Members' Fridays because there was an all-night sitting. There was only one Friday dedicated to private Members' bills remaining; and two other bills—one on taxi-cabs and one on ice-cream—had precedence over it. If the debate on those bills should take up the whole day, Herbert's bill would lapse. They in fact did so. But fortunately for Herbert, Baldwin, the Prime Minister, decided to give him an extra day and the bill got its Third Reading by 190 votes to 37.

There remained then only the Lords. The Lords, which in the past was on political matters so often obstructive to the reforming plans of the Commons, has often in recent years shown itself on social questions more ready for change than the other House. It met with no difficulty there except that the Lords changed the period of five years which was necessary before a petitioner could sue for divorce to three years. Herbert was afraid that the opponents of his bill might take advantage of this, when the bill came back to the Commons, to delay its passage. However they did not do so and the bill passed safely on to the Statute Book.

If recently it was—and indeed still is—a common cause

of complaint that the private back-bencher never has an opportunity of carrying a bill, now, a little perversely, when he has shown that with pertinacity he can obtain some results (whether for good or ill), some are heard to complain that it is irresponsible of Government to leave such matters to private initiative, and that it should have the courage to take and impose its own decisions.

The Labour Government of 1964–70 offered considerable assistance to the private Members who promoted bills on such matters as abortion, homosexual law reform, divorce and capital punishment, mainly by providing parliamentary time. The Conservative Government elected in 1970 has said that it will not assist private Members' bills in this way, but it has recently agreed that the Members who win the top places in the ballot should be given a sum of money for expert drafting assistance.

2

Government Legislation

Yet by far the greater number of laws and the more important laws passed today are laws passed by the Government, introduced into the House by the relevant minister and carried on division by the vote of Government supporters, shepherded into the lobby by the Government Whips.

A bill, whether it be a private or a public bill (see p. 132), begins with a First Reading. The Clerk reads out from a dummy the title of the bill and it is ordered to be printed. This is the procedure on all bills except the annual financial bills which are founded on resolutions of the House. In medieval times, before printing, the First Reading was a real reading, and the Speaker then read out the bill to the House. Now it is a mere formality and involves only a licence to print the bill.

At the First Reading a day is appointed for the Second

Reading, which is the first crucial stage of the bill. The Second Reading is a general debate on the broad principles of the bill. The bill will be introduced by its proposer—if a Government bill, by the minister in charge of it. He will make a speech. He will then be followed by the leading Opposition front-bench speaker. At the end of the debate the question is put and the Opposition, if it so wishes, challenges a division. A money resolution is then passed authorising the payment of any money that may be involved by the bill. This is seldom challenged.

The changes in the constitution of the House of Commons and in the nature of the legislation which it passes have over the years been considerable. But the changes in procedure have on the whole been remarkably small. A bill today is passed in very much the same way as it was passed in the reign of Charles I and indeed, in so far as we can trace it, not very differently even from what it was before the time of the Tudors. 'The Parliamentary procedure of 1844', wrote Sir R. Palgrave in his Preface to the tenth edition of Erskine May, 'was essentially the procedure on which the House of Commons conducted its business during the Long Parliament.' And though it has changed, it has not changed very much even since. Sir Thomas Smith, Queen Elizabeth's Secretary of State, explained the procedure as it was in his day. 'All bills be thrice, on three divers days, read and disputed upon before they come to the question. After the bill hath been twice read and then engrossed, and eftsoons read and disputed upon enough as is thought, the Speaker asketh if they will go to the question. It chanceth sometimes that some part of the bill is allowed, some other part hath much doubt and contrariety made of it, and it is thought if it were amended it would go forward. They then choose certain committees of them which have spoken with the bill and against it to amend it and bring it in again so amended, as they amongst them shall think meet; and this is before it is engrossed, yea and sometimes, after. But the agreement of these committees is no prejudice to the House. For at the last question they will either accept it or dash it as it shall seem good, notwithstanding that whatsoever the committees have done.'

If the bill is defeated on Second Reading that, of course, means that the House wishes to see no more of it and that is the end of it. But with the Government being by definition in a majority and with the Whips on, this very rarely happens. The excitement of the division is as a rule merely to see whether the majority is slightly less or slightly greater than that expected, owing to a few odd abstentions. An abstention on a division is tolerated. To vote against the party is considered a much more serious matter. If, as is usual, the bill survives its Second Reading it then goes for consideration clause by clause and detail by detail to committee, either upstairs to one of the standing committees already described, or to a Committee of the Whole House on the floor of the House. Thence it emerges, probably amended in certain details, and is reported back to the House. Members are presented with a newly printed version of it in its amended form and the House decides on Report whether to accept or to reject the amendments which the committee has made. After the Report stage there is the Third Reading. There the question to accept the bill is put without debate unless six Members have given written notice that they want a debate. If and when the Third Reading is passed, then the House of Commons has for the moment finished with the bill. It goes up to the Lords. (Bills affecting Scotland are remitted to the Scottish Grand Committee on which all Scottish Members sit and where it receives what is virtually its Second Reading. The committee stage is taken in the Scottish Standing Committee.)

The procedure in the Lords is basically the same as that in the Commons. The only difference is that amendments are less restricted. Amendments are generally of two kinds. There are the amendments made by private peers to satisfy their own opinions or their own dislikes of the bill as it is presented to them. In view of the admittedly subordinate nature of the Lords, these amendments are more often moved than passed or voted on. The Lords, of course, would always have the power to vote down any Government bill—particularly, in view of their Conservative majority, one that came from a Labour House of Commons. But no purpose would be served by challenging constant confrontations with the Commons. Such amendments therefore are generally used by peers merely as a method of giving advertisement to their views. The other type of amendment made in the Lords consists of amendments made by the minister either to fulfil a promise that has been made during the course of the bill's previous debates or to clear up some drafting confusion that has emerged. In general, procedure in the Lords is more leisurely than in the Commons and the Lords usually take the committee stage in the full House, but the pressure of business is compelling even the Lords to remit some committee stages to standing committees.

If the Lords make no amendments then once the bill has passed through its third Reading there, Parliament has finished with it and nothing remains for it but to receive the royal assent. If it has been amended by the Lords then it goes back in its amended form to the Commons and it is for the Commons to decide whether to agree or to disagree with the Lords' amendments. Generally in modern times if the House of Commons disagrees with the Lords, the Lords, having made their protest, bow to the Commons. If they show themselves obstinate, informal conversations will take place between the representatives of both Houses to see if an acceptable compromise can be reached. But there is no constitutional machinery compelling the one House to give way to the other. If they refuse to agree, then the bill cannot pass into law unless and until it has passed a second time through the Commons in exactly the same form and is thus able to qualify for the royal assent under the Parliament Act without the Lords' assent.

Private Bills and Delegated Legislation

Private bills are different in their nature from public bills. The private bill (quite a different thing from the private Member's bill) is not a bill designed to change the general law of the land. It is a bill which proposes to change the law in some particular place or as it applies to some particular persons. Acts which arise from a private bill are called local and private acts. Before a private bill is introduced notice must be given to the people who are to be affected by it. Estimates of the amount of money that will be involved must be made. All this work—the work of seeing that the standing orders are complied with—are in the hands of officers known as examiners. The bill cannot be introduced until the examiners are satisfied. The bill then introduced, it is open to the House to refuse it a Second Reading, but this is not often done unless it is felt that the bill goes beyond its proposed narrow purpose and trenches on some matter of general principle. Normally, the bill will be referred to the Private Bill Committee. The bill has a preamble to explain why its introduction is thought desirable. The first duty of the committee is to consider whether it is satisfied by this preamble. If satisfied, the committee goes through its clause in a committee stage to which expert counsel and witnesses may be summoned and cross-examined and then reports it, amended or unamended as the case may be, to the House. The bill has to be given a report and Third Reading as with any other bill. The difference between a private and public bill is not so much in the procedure as that the great majority of private bills are on local and administrative matters and arouse no opposition. The public bill has to be carried through in a single session. If it fails in that, it lapses and all its processes have to begin again, if its supporters persist in it, at the next session. With private bills, since they are so often on matters of administration which arouse no controversies, it is the custom, if they are not completed, to allow them to be carried on into the next session. Very occasionally bills after their Second Reading are sent to a small select committee or to a joint committee of both Houses. This is done on certain highly technical bills.

The number of private bills in recent years has been in steady decrease. Such matters as social welfare, public health, water works, new railways and the like were in Victorian times dealt with by specific private bills. In modern times it has become increasingly the habit to allow such matters to be regulated by provisional orders or special orders. The Ministry now issues special orders after the publication of notices in the locality affected or perhaps after a local inquiry.

Parliament is sovereign and can always recall any powers that it may have delegated to other bodies. Nevertheless in fact the greater number of regulations to which we give obedience in our daily life are not the direct commands of Parliament but the commands of bodies or persons to whom Parliament has delegated authority. This has always been so to some extent, and in the complexity of modern life it is so today to a much greater extent than ever before. Delegations are broadly of two sorts. Parliament gives authority to the minister to make regulations of certain sorts and within certain limits. Or it gives authority to other bodies to exercise certain powers. For instance, it gives certain specified authorities to county councils, city councils and other municipal bodies. It gives, as we have said, powers to the Church Assembly or the Synod of the Church of England. Until recent changes it gave special powers, subject to its own overriding authority, to the Parliament of Northern Ireland at Stormont.

Widespread powers to make regulations on details are given in numerous acts to various ministers. It is hard to see how the country could be governed by any other procedure. There are those who, as we have already said, argue that the remedy lies in Parliament regulating less. It may be possible to reduce a little bit the volume of legislation, and it might be desirable to do so, but, whatever reductions are made, it is certain that our society is such that the volume of legislation would remain far too large to be completely covered by positive Acts of Parliament. A good deal of delegation is inevitable. Parliament has a certain control, or pretence of control, over such Statutory Instruments as they are called. They may by Parliament's will be subject to affirmative or to negative resolutions. If they are subject to affirmative resolutions, they have to receive a positive vote of the House before they can come into force. If they are subject to negative resolutions, it is open to the House within a certain time, usually within forty days, to pray against the Instrument and, if a majority can be induced to vote against it, it is annulled. Or it can be decided that all that is required is to lay the Instrument before Parliament so that Parliament is at least aware of its existence. There are committees in both Houses to examine Statutory Instruments, and those committees do valuable work in calling attention to drafting confusions in the Instrument or to exercises of power more sweeping than those which the parent act authorised. They can advise the House what Instruments are of sufficient importance to make it worth while praying against them. But the actual debates on the prayers are not perhaps of very great value. They take place late at night after the ordinary business of the day has been completed. They are therefore too late to catch the next morning's newspapers. They are not usually on matters of general interest. The Whips are on and therefore, with few exceptions, the result of the vote is the usual foregone conclusion. It is only possible to approve or reject the Instrument. There is no possibility of amending it. With the growing complexity of modern life the number of such Instruments has steadily increased; and their increase, whether or not it is inevitable, has aroused in some people considerable alarm.

4
The Ombudsman

The Ombudsman was an officer imported into this country in 1967 from the examples of Sweden, Denmark and New Zealand. His official title in this country is the Parliamentary Commissioner for Administration. His task is to investigate complaints of maladministration, but he is precluded from concerning himself with matters affecting the armed services, police, hospitals, the local authorities or the nationalised industries. Critics have argued that these restrictions are so great as to rob the post of effectiveness. But in the first thirty-three months of his existence he found, according to his report, that, out of 864 cases investigated, in 105 some measure of maladministration requiring remedy was discovered. Perhaps the most notable of his cases up to the present is the Sachsenhausen case. Twelve persons who had been during the war interned in Sachsenhausen concentration camp claimed that they had been wrongfully refused compensation due to them by the Foreign Office. The Foreign Office asserted that they had not been imprisoned under concentration camp conditions. The Ombudsman decided that the Foreign Office had based its conclusions on 'partial and largely irrelevant information'. A debate took place on February 5, 1968. The Foreign Secretary rejected the criticism but announced that further grants would be made to the complainants out of respect for the Ombudsman. The Select Committee on the Parliamentary Commissioner for Administration was, however, not content with this, but insisted on repeating the Ombudsman's criticism of the Foreign Office officials. They thus established a very important principle. The traditional theory was that the minister must take responsibility for all the acts of the

135

officials of his department. In simpler days when the department did little and when the civil servants comprised no more than a handful of the minister's private servants, that was well enough. The tradition survived up till more recent times even though by then the ministers no longer had, or could have, knowledge of the details of what civil servants did in his name. For instance when in 1954 the scandal about the release of land from service occupation on Crichel Down came to light, Sir Thomas Dugdale, the minister, insisted on resigning though he knew nothing of the case. The Sachsenhausen case established a new principle that responsibility could be pinned on the civil service officials.

The Government has announced that separate Ombudsmen are to be created to cover the fields of local government and the National Health service.

VI

FINANCE

Parliament came into existence because kings, anxious for adventurous policies which could not be financed out of their own resources, appealed to their subjects for more money. The first business of the House of Commons was to give or withhold money from the King and, as a condition of doing so, it insisted on a redress of its grievances. As long as the Executive was really the King's Executive, Parliament's control of governmental expenditure was very real. Today, with the Executive dependent not on the choice of the Sovereign but on that of Parliament, the situation is very different. Members still often enough make rounded speeches calling for government economy in general but, when it comes to details, their demands are always for more government expenditure—more generous pensions and the like—and the chances of the House refusing the Government some expenditure which it demands are almost negligible.

As Erskine May puts it, 'the Crown demands money, the Commons grant it and the Lords assent to the grant'. Up till the disputes of the seventeenth century and the Civil War the Commons had indeed the right to grant or to withhold direct taxation, but there were a number of other indirect ways in which the Sovereign could raise money with or without challenge and thus could, if with difficulty, carry on his government for a considerable time without summoning Parliament. The whole position was only finally put beyond argument by the Bill of Rights of 1688 which said that 'levying money for, or to the use of,

the Crown by pretence of prerogative without grant of
Parliament for longer time or in other manner than the
same is, or shall be granted, is illegal'. Previously Parliament had granted the Sovereign 'aids and supplies' without specifying in detail on what purpose the money was to
be spent. After William III's accession, the international
situation was such that it was necessary to maintain a
standing army. The memories of Cromwell made such an
army highly unpopular. All that Parliament was willing to
vote was an annual Mutiny Act, providing money for the
support of an army and navy for one year, and this act
had to be, and was, renewed year after year but always for
one year only.

Also from Charles II's time onwards, instead of allowing the King a private income with which, at any rate in
peaceful times, he could live of his own, Parliament took
from him all the revenue which would enable him to
maintain the Government's expenditure and instead gave
him a Civil List of his own—an income which he could
spend on his own private purposes. The money raised by
taxation was not only to be spent on governmental purposes in general but also earmarked for specific purposes,
and committees were set up to see that the money was
spent on the purpose for which it was voted. These small
committees were not in these early times very effective,
and the control of expenditure fell into the hands of the
whole House of Commons sitting as a committee—into
the hands of the Committee of the Whole House. There
were two committees—the Committee of Supply and the
Committee of Ways and Means. They were committees in
name only, for all Members of Parliament belonged to
them. The only advantage which they had over a full
meeting of the House was that they met under the chair-
manship of the Chairman of Ways and Means, who was
the House's own nominee, rather than of the Speaker, who
was suspect as the King's man. Yet even when the control
of the purse had passed completely into the hands of
Parliament, the custom was still preserved, as it had been
in truly monarchical days, that the Crown—that is to say

by now the ministers—alone had the right to propose a tax. The House had the right to reduce it but not to increase it. The condition was specifically asserted in Standing Order No. 8 of 1706. 'This House will receive no petition for any sum relating to public service or proceed upon any motion for a grant or charge upon the public revenue . . . unless recommended from the Crown.' Parliament is sovereign, and there is of course nothing to prevent it from at any time repealing this Standing Order, but it has never done so and the private Member lives under this self-denying ordinance to this day.

What is the purpose of it? It was, to begin with, certainly a safeguard against corruption. It was thought that if Members could vote additional sums of money they would vote them to themselves and their friends. Members fell into the habit of voting for a special purpose more money than was needed: there was then a surplus to be distributed and this surplus was distributed among 'petitioners'. Today corruption would be doubtless less crude, but it is still possible to corrupt the mass of voters by the voting of bread and circuses in one way or another. To put such a temptation into the hands of a private Member who would have no responsibility for the general finances of the nation would, it was thought, be too dangerous. A Chancellor of the Exchequer, having to answer for the general effect of his policies, will be more responsible. The argument is coherent. But it means that the influence of the back-bencher over financial policy is little more than nominal, for it is not possible for him to advocate more than trivial changes of taxation, since to every proposed change the Chancellor can convincingly answer that the money must be found somewhere. If it is not to be raised in this way, in what way can it be raised? And on the answer to that question the private Member is not allowed to say anything.

What real control of expenditure, then, is there? Every year the Government lays before Parliament estimates to cover the whole range of its civil and military programme. These estimates are grouped into twelve classes. The votes on all these classes were in the nineteenth century brought forward separately in succession. The House debated them. Members could move amendments. If it wished, the House could reject a vote, though since the votes were Government votes and the Whips were on, this very rarely happened. With the second half of the century, Supply-day debates quite changed their nature. The estimates were still open to debate but those debates became less inquisitions into the actual expenditure of the department, which was now too complicated a task to be usefully performed in a series of speeches in general debate of the whole House. Today a number of days—not less than twenty-nine—before August 5 must be devoted to Supply. The subject of the Supply debates is, by convention, at the selection of the Opposition—that is to say, in fact at the selection of the Opposition front bench. The back-bench Opposition member has little say in such selections except in so far as he can bring pressure to bear on his leaders by representation in private party committees upstairs. The debate is usually a general debate on some aspects of a department's policy—not merely its financial administration. Balfour explained the modern position in a speech of 1896: 'While Supply does not exist for the purpose of enforcing economy on the Government, it does exist for the purpose of criticising the policy of the Government, of controlling their administration and bringing them to book for their policy at home and abroad.' The only Supply days that are today used for genuine discussion of the expenditure of money are the debates on the reports of the Public Accounts Committee or the Expenditure Committee.

Life is complicated by the confusion of the calendar. The general calendar year begins in January. The sessional year begins in October, and the financial year begins in April. There is therefore a good deal of overlapping. In February the main estimates, civil and military, for the coming year are presented to the House. At the same time the House passes a Vote on Account of a third of these estimates—that being, as is reckoned, a sufficient sum to carry on until the full Finance Bill consequent on the Budget has passed into law and received the royal assent.

The House, of course, still has to vote supplies but the voting of supplies is now separated from the debate on Supply. The voting of Supply takes place after the conclusion of a Supply Debate. The control over the sums proposed, in so far as there is any control at all, is no longer really in the hands of the House but in the hands of relevant committees. The Estimates Committee was revived in 1921. Its duty was to consider whether the sums voted could be more efficiently administered. It had no authority to criticise the total amount of the estimates. But it was able in 1958 to call into question the whole theory of the Treasury's control of expenditure. It was this challenge which led to the appointment of the Plowden Committee which overhauled the whole method of Treasury control. Treasury consent under the present system has to be won by every other department before its estimates are approved; and it has been argued that such a system was well adapted to a Gladstonian economy, when the prime purpose was to keep Government expenditure as low as possible, but it is very ill suited for any economy which calls for positive social policies. The present arrangement has come under a good deal of criticism, most vigorously perhaps from Mr. Max Nicholson in his book, *The System*. Treasury officials, he says, are 'ill trained, incompetent and unfitted for their jobs'. The fault lies with the educational system from which they are produced—the classical education as fashioned by Benjamin Jowett, the Master of Balliol of the last century. We need not follow Mr. Nicholson into his disquisitions against a classical education, which take us a little beyond our argument, nor into his alternative remedy of business government which awakens ideas that are ominously reminiscent of Horatio Bottomley. He pleads for decentralisation and gives not very happily as an example— Northern Ireland. But, however that may be, Lord Plowden has amply shown that the relationship calls urgently for review, as was again shown by the inquiry into the constitution of the civil service which the Estimates Committee also instituted in 1964–5.

In 1970 the House reconstituted an Expenditure Committee which has wider power since it need not confine itself to an investigation of the expenditure of the votes but can give its opinion on the nature and volume of future expenditure. Yet so long as we preserve the traditional British system at all, the limited powers of all such committees is inevitable. In the last resort, supposing a Chancellor sees fit to reject their criticisms, the matter must be remitted to the vote of the whole House, and there, since he will have the power of the Whips behind him, he will presumably be able to carry the day whether or not he has the better of the argument.

The auditing of Public Accounts was for many years haphazard. The committees appointed in the eighteenth century were, as has been said, ineffective, and the Committee of the Whole House even more so. In 1785 an act appointed regular commissioners for auditing the accounts, and a further act in 1802 established Finance Accounts commissioners whose duty it was to lay before Parliament an overall statement of national accounts. Even then these statements did not show actual accounts but only the issues made by the Treasury to various departments. It was not until 1869 that complete accounts were laid before Parliament. In 1861 a Committee of Public Accounts of the House of Commons was established, and in 1866 an independent Comptroller and Auditor-General. These two reforms established the system of financial scrutiny substantially as it has remained until today. It has in recent years from time to time given examples of its efficiency. For instance in 1964 it brought to light the excessive profits which Ferranti Ltd. had made from the supply of guided missiles, and in 1965 the profit of Bristol Siddeley Engines from the overhaul of their engines.

If we ask how far in modern times the control of finance is effective, we can say that the control of the manner of expenditure is on the whole effective, exercised by the Public Accounts Committee and the Auditor-General and

Comptroller General. Any minister who spent money that had not been voted would be called to account—though not, it is true, until after the money had been already spent and when it might not be possible to recover it. On the other hand, the control over the amount that is raised is not very real.

As to the actual machinery of Parliamentary control of the nation's finances, the major taxes are of course permanent. The only question about, say, the income tax is whether it will be slightly raised or lowered. The sort of hopes that were entertained at the time of the Crimean War, that it would be only a temporary tax, are of course of no reality. All money is nevertheless only voted for a year.

The money, once voted by Parliament and collected, is paid into the Bank of England by whom it is held in what is known as the Consolidated Fund. Before 1787 when Pitt introduced this reform, particular taxes had to be earmarked for a particular purpose. That is no longer so. Expenditure is of two kinds: the regular expenditure demanded by standing laws, and the annual appropriations for a particular service. Of the expenditure regulated by standing laws—which are known as payments made out of the Consolidated Fund—the most important are those to meet the charges of the National Debt. These are expenditures which could not be avoided save by an act of national bankruptcy. Then there is the Civil List—the money necessary to defray the expenses of the royal family. It is the custom to settle the size of the Civil List at the beginning of each reign, which means of course, as seems to be happening at the moment, that if the Soveriegn should reign through a period of inflation and rising prices, she is after a time in considerable difficulty and probably has to ask for a revision of the amount of the Civil List. The Debt is of various sorts. There are the funded debts of which the State is under obligation to make a payment at fixed interest rates unless and until it repays the principle at par. The unfunded debt which includes the floating debt, Treasury bills, ways and means advances and temporary borrowings from the banks are repayable within fixed periods. Apart from these debts there are certain capital liabilities—loans which the State has undertaken for certain purposes. The lenders to the State and the taxpayers are in these days so nearly the same persons, so many people hold War Loans and the like, that the operation of meeting the National Debt is very largely an operation of taking money out of the citizen's right-hand pocket and replacing it in the left.

Any grant made by Parliament for the service of a particular year lapses, if it is not spent by the end of the financial year—that is by March 31. Within fifteen days after the end of the financial year the Treasury is required by an Act of 1873 to prepare an account of the public income and expenditure of the previous year. If it is found that there was a deficit the deficit must be made good in the following year. If there was a surplus the surplus is handed over to the National Debt Commissioners and put into a sinking fund, to be used for the redemption of debt. The duty of the Comptroller and Auditor-General is to make sure that all public money is spent in accordance with the purpose for which it was appropriated. He is a permanent official with his expenses and salary paid out of the Consolidated Fund and not a party politician who goes in or out with changing Governments.

The various spending departments prepare towards the end of the calendar year their estimates of the money which they will require for the coming year. These estimates are sent in to the Treasury and scrutinised by them. There is, as we have said, at the present a good deal of criticism of the manner of Treasury control. Whatever the merits of that criticism, the system still stands for the moment that, after the Treasury scrutiny, the estimates are submitted to the Cabinet, by whom the decision of appropriation is taken. The Sovereign's speech at the opening of Parliament has given a general statement of the policies which the Government is proposing to pursue and, as soon as possible after the Sovereign's speech, estimates of the cost of those policies are laid before the House of

Commons (though not before the Lords). In time of war, when for security reasons it is not possible to publish exact figures of estimates, the House passes general notes of credit in round figures for the Army, the Navy, the Air Force and civil services.

One of the first tasks of the House, after the voting of the Sovereign's speech, used to be to set up two committees, the Committee of Supply and the Committee of Ways and Means—both Committees of the Whole House. The duty of the Committee of Supply was to vote such money as may be required, that of the Committee of Ways and Means to vote the taxes necessary for raising it. These committees date back to the time of Charles I. At that time the House would consider in one committee how much money it would grant the Sovereign for a particular purpose and in another how it would allow the money for that purpose to be raised. At the present time the debates of the Committee of Supply, as has been said, are not concerned with financial measures. The Committee of Supply has lost its raison d'être, and it was abolished on December 14, 1966. When at last all the accounts of the various departments have been passed by the House of Commons they are submitted to the Auditor-General. They are then submitted to the Committee of Public Accounts which considers in detail whether the money has been properly spent.

Once a year, some time around Easter and soon after the completion of the financial year, the Chancellor of the Exchequer introduces his Budget in which he gives the House an account of the financial state of the nation and announces the changes in taxation which he proposes for the coming year. His proposals are put into the form of resolutions which are handed in to the chair immediately after the Chancellor has finished his Budget speech. Budget resolutions are immediately put and usually given unanimous acceptance. This is to enable the relevant taxes to be immediately levied so as to prevent the public from taking advantage by purchasing in quantity some article which the Budget statement has shown will be going up in a few day's time. But the tax changes have not got full legal effect until they have been embodied in an Act of Parliament. If by any chance a levy envisaged by the Chancellor in his Budget statement is withdrawn in the debates of the subsequent Finance Bill, the money collected under this resolution is refunded.

After the Budget statement—which is only a statement of intent—a Finance Bill is presented to the House. In it all the details of taxation for the coming year are embodied and the House goes through it clause by clause, considering such amendments as the Chairman of Committees selects, and, at the conclusion of debate on each clause, passes a motion that 'the clause (or the clause as amended) do stand part'. The debate on the Finance Bill always occupies a number of days, and it is for Members a tiresome and frustrating occasion. What matters of principle the Budget may embody have already been discussed in the general Budget debate. This is concerned only with details. The rule for the adjournment of the debate at a fixed hour is suspended for financial business. Therefore the Finance Bill debates are almost certain to involve Members in a few all-night sittings—always an intensely disagreeable affair. A few Members take part in the farce. The great majority hang about in the library, the smoking-room or one of the bars. From time to time the division bell rings and they troop in to record their votes in the lobby to which their Whip directs them. In the course of the debate the Chancellor may make a few concessions but very few. For he has obviously already made up his mind before introducing his Budget in what ways he is going to raise his revenue. Any considerable or important concession would throw out of balance his whole economy. Therefore, however urgent or cogent the arguments that the Opposition may advance, they are very much more often than not met by a stern negative which the Chancellor's party colleagues, most of whom have not heard the debate and most probably do not know what is the matter at issue, obediently support in the division lobby. When on April 24, 1972, a new clause was added to the Housing

Bill against the wishes of the Government, the Government at once reversed the decision by making the House refuse to agree that the clause which had been voted only a few minutes before do stand part of the bill.

If the decision about the future of the nation were really taken, and not merely nominally taken, in this manner by exhausted Members, half drunk with sleep, at 3.30 in the morning, no sane man would tolerate the system. They only tolerate it because the decision is not really taken by Members in an all-night sitting but has already been taken by wide-awake Treasury officials, now seated listening in the box as the debate drags on. This is well enough for the Treasury officials, and the public, which is only interested in the result, in a manner accepts it. But it is hard on the Members, called on to do their work, to quote George Trevelyan, 'at an hour when all honest men should be in bed, at an hour when, if we are to believe some cynics, all honest men are in bed'.

Until the middle of the nineteenth century the Government used to bring in separate bills for separate taxes. In accordance with this practice, Gladstone in 1860 brought in a bill to repeal the paper duty. The Lords rejected it. Therefore, to make the Lords' interference more difficult, Gladstone in 1861 brought in a composite bill, including all the taxation proposals of the year, and this practice has been followed ever since. The general custom has been to have only one single annual Budget, but there have been plenty of occasions in these times of difficulty when a second Budget in the autumn has been found necessary.

The Government raises money by taxation. It also raises it by loan. The Government borrows to meet expenses for which the tax revenue has not yet come in or for special expenditure that cannot reasonably be met out of the current receipts of the year. Every Consolidated Fund Act gives the Government power to raise more short-term loans by Treasury bills. When in 1909 the Lords rejected the Finance Bill, it was by means of these Treasury bills that the nation's business was carried on. For long-term loans special legislation is needed.

Originally, as we have said, the primary business of Parliament was to decide whether the King should be granted the money that he needed to carry through his policy. If it refused him the money the policy had to be abandoned, or the King had to find some devious way of getting money. This, in the days when Parliament and the King were in conflict, was a really effective control. Today, when the King's ministers are the men who have the support of the majority of the House, the control is not very real. With present-day strict party discipline it is highly unlikely that the House would revolt and refuse the Chancellor measures for taxation which he demanded. The Chancellor has only to stand firm and he can carry the day immediately on the floor of the House. This does not mean that all debate in the House is purposeless. Members can sometimes mobilise public opinion against a proposal—possibly even cause the Chancellor to withdraw it rather than incur odium for his Government. But it must be confessed that the newspapers and television are increasingly developing the habit of reporting the Chancellor's original proposals as if they were already law and their enactment an unimportant formality.

In recent years it has become increasingly common to give to the Chancellor a power of delegated taxation. The first example of this was in the Import Duties Act of 1932. In 1948 the Chancellor was given power to vary the classification of goods subject to purchase tax, and 1961 saw the introduction of the regulator giving the Chancellor authority to move up or down the rates of purchase tax.

Until 1968, the committee stage of the Finance Bill was always taken on the floor of the House. In that year, the whole bill was sent to a standing committee, against furious protests from the Opposition. In 1969 a compromise was introduced whereby some of its clauses were considered on the floor of the House and the more technical details by a standing committee upstairs.

Some other countries—France for instance and Germany before the war, so long as she remained a Parliamentary country—put real power into the hands of finance committees. There are those who advocate the establishment of such form of financial control in this country. The general verdict is that the evils of them would greatly outweigh their benefits. Committees may have their useful role to fulfil but the Government cannot be master of the nation's policy if it is not master of its finances. Kings discovered that in the days when they were still trying to fight for power against Parliament. And therefore the final say, if there is to be an effective policy, must rest with the Chancellor. The question is not really so much whether the Chancellor must rule as whether, so long as he rules, Parliamentary Government can be more than a façade. Recent attempts to divide responsibility between an Economics Minister and the traditional Chancellor have not been very successful.

VII

PARLIAMENT AND FOREIGN AFFAIRS

Parliament's relation to foreign policy is somewhat different from that to domestic policy. British customs know nothing of definite regulations (such as obtain in the United States) about the signature of treaties, or the declaration of war, by Parliament. The United Kingdom has never declared any of its wars as a result of a formal vote of Parliament. The Executive can act in its foreign relations by royal prerogative—that is to say, has a right to act without formal approval of Parliament. Nevertheless, in the Labour Government of 1923 Lord Ponsonby, then Under-Secretary for Foreign Affairs, laid down what is called the Ponsonby rule by which the Government agreed not to ratify any treaty for a period of twenty-one days after its signature, during which time Parliament would have the opportunity to debate it. What is the exact authority of this rule, indeed why it is called a rule at all, is far from clear. Lord Ponsonby was only an Under-Secretary and had no sort of authority to make rules of procedure. If Parliament should vote against a treaty which the Government has signed, presumably the treaty would not be ratified and the Government would fall, but such a thing has never yet happened.

Yet, though there may not be a need for formal legislation and though there is no formal House of Commons' Committee on Foreign Affairs similar to the American, Members—particularly in modern times—contrive to keep a very close eye on foreign policy. They do this by regular questioning of the Foreign Secretary and his

Under-Secretaries. In a crisis it is always open to a Member to ask a special-notice question. Matters of foreign affairs can be raised in the adjournment debates. There are debates on specific issues, sometimes emergency debates for which the House is especially recalled—as happened at the time of the Russian invasion of Czechoslovakia in 1968. There are also general debates on foreign affairs, usually spaced over two or three days. These are apt to be somewhat unsatisfactory since different Members wish to discuss different issues and the debates lack unity. It works out that the equivalent of about one day in every fifteen is spent on the discussion of foreign policy. Although the Government does not require the authority of explicit legislation for its action as in domestic affairs, the control of Parliament over foreign policy is of course complete. It would be quite impossible for a Government to sustain a foreign policy for which it had not the support of Parliament, and if the Government proposed any action of moment it would have to obtain the vote of Parliament. The Suez story indicated that it was probably not possible for a Government to carry through a policy of war unless it also had the support of the Opposition.

If in fact no Government policy has been prevented in modern times by Parliamentary action, that is due no doubt to some extent to the vigour of the Whips who, in this as in other matters, are energetic in containing rebellion. But the power of the Whips is not unlimited. They could not obtain support for policies of which Members deeply disapproved. Chamberlain's Government in 1940 was not actually defeated in the House of Commons but the revolt of a very substantial proportion of his supporters was such that it was not possible for him to continue in power. In the debate on the entry into the European Community there have been revolts against party discipline in both parties but, when the division was on the real merits of the question, it was found that there were many more Labour Members prepared to vote for our entry than there were Conservatives to vote against it. Mr. Heath and his Government had a comfortable majority.

It was only when the vote became a merely party vote, almost irrespective of the merits of the question, that the majority was narrow. But the general lesson is that, keen as is the interest of many Members in foreign affairs, differing as they do from one another in opinions and ready, as many Members are, to criticise even the policies of their own party, the issues are not generally considered sufficient for Members to bring down a Government on them; but because the urgency for a foreign policy rises and falls with circumstances, it is always possible that an issue will arise so grave that Members are prepared to desert their party and upset the Government. On the other hand, quite apart from Parliamentary advantage, a sensible Government sees the importance of not committing the country to foreign policies which are not supported in the country, whether inside or outside Parliament. Such a crisis has therefore not arisen.

Debates on foreign affairs are also from time to time held in the House of Lords. These debates rarely if ever lead to a division, and the fate of the Government is not in question. But they are often of very great value. The Lords contain a number of ex-ambassadors and others who have held important posts abroad. They usually belong to no political party and do not take part in the ordinary party battles. But they are able from their independent experience very often to pass valuable judgement on the development of events.

VIII

THE GROWTH OF

PARLIAMENTARY DEMOCRACY

People sometimes speak as if Parliamentary sovereignty and democratic government were one and the same thing and almost interchangeable terms. It is far from so. We have had Parliaments, and to some extent Parliamentary sovereignty, in this country for many centuries. By the widest stretch of the word we cannot be said to have had democratic government any longer than since 1885, and even for many years after that the franchise was only a male franchise and not of 'One man one vote'. Men of property were allowed to vote in every constituency in which they happened to own property.

In 1254 Henry III, in great need of money, demanded of the sheriff of every county that he choose two knights to meet together and consider what assistance they would give the King. These knights were representatives of all the freemen of their county and not merely of the King's tenants. Eleven years later there met Simon de Montfort's Parliament, which is commonly spoken of as England's first Parliament. To it were summoned not only knights from the shires but also representatives of the cities and boroughs. The later form of Parliament was clearly established by the Model Parliament which Edward I summoned in 1295. To it he summoned all the archbishops, bishops and greater abbots—also seven earls and forty-one barons. The archbishops and bishops were directed to bring with them the heads of their cathedral chapters, their archdeacons, one proctor for the cathedral clergy and two proctors for the clergy of the diocese. From the laity the sheriffs were directed to select two knights from each shire, two citizens from each city and two burgesses from each borough.

The Model Parliament was for the first time a national body which was in no way a mere feudal assembly. Edward's Parliament was intended to be a tri-partite assembly of the three orders—the clergy, the nobility and the Commons—after the model of the French *tiers état*. Before the end of the fourteenth century, Parliament had already established its two fundamental principles: that the King had no right to impose direct taxation without its consent, and had only the right to impose such indirect taxes as were specifically recognised by the Great Charter.

As the bulk of the money was forthcoming from the Commons, this arrangement involved the recognition of the Commons as more important than the Lords. The King looked for support for his policies both to Lords and Commons. The people who handled the cash and were able to supply it to the King for his wars were the merchants in the towns, the burghers, the Commons. In 1407 Henry agreed that money grants should be initiated by the Commons and only reported to the Sovereign when they had been accepted by both Houses. So long as he received the rights to tunnage and poundage (that is, to collect the custom dues) for life he was in a fairly independent position, but after the deposition of Richard II, Parliament only granted this right to Henry IV for a limited time. He was in consequence more firmly subordinate to his Parliament than any of his predecessors. But after the Battle of Agincourt Parliament, in a fit of enthusiasm, made the grant of tunnage and poundage to Henry V for life and it was granted to Henry VI and all his successors up to the time of the quarrels of Parliament with the Stuart kings.

To begin with there was only one house of Parliament, Lords and Commons met together. It was when they started to tax themselves in different ways that they tended to split up, and the Commons inevitably then became the more important. How the Commons were to be constituted was in these early days very uncertainly defined. 'The Commons,' says Stubbs, 'are the communities, the organised bodies of freemen of the shires and towns, and the estate of the Commons is the general body into which for the purposes of Parliament, these communities are combined.' In the counties it was the duty of the sheriff to cause a selection to be made of two knights for each shire, but no attempt was made to lay down for him whom he was to consult nor how they were to be selected. It was not until 1430, in Henry VI's reign, that any attempt was made to lay down definite conditions of election. An act was then passed to prevent riots at elections. In order to achieve that purpose it was enacted that the vote in counties should be exercisable by freeholders who held a property of a value of forty shillings. This continued to be the qualification for four hundred years up to the Reform Bill of 1832.

If there was a certain regulation of the county franchise there was no regulation at all of the borough franchise. The sheriff was commanded to provide for two members to be sent to Parliament from each borough but given no instruction as to what constituted a borough. There was in these early days no general ambition to be a Member of Parliament and no general desire by towns to be recognised as boroughs. The journey to London and Parliament was onerous and expensive. The boroughs themselves were under obligation to pay the expenses of those who went to represent them. Very often they would rather not be represented at all and were only too glad to make an arrangement with the sheriff not to recognise them as boroughs. But in the sixteenth century—and particularly in Elizabeth's reign—the new policy was developed of creating new boroughs or towns over whose representation the Sovereign thought that she would have control. Henry VIII created thirty-eight constituencies among which were the Welsh constituencies, which in his reign for the first time returned Members to the House. Elizabeth created sixty-two. The Queen was Duke of Cornwall, owner of the land, and able to nominate the burgesses who would represent Cornish constituencies. No part of the country in the years before the Reform bill provided more scandalous little rotten boroughs than Cornwall, and these were mostly the creation of Elizabeth, who contrived to fill the House of Commons with safe men dependent on her for their membership. This habit of creating new boroughs of royal character was largely discontinued in the next century and was completely discontinued after the reign of Charles II. Charles II's creation of Newark was the last creation of a royal borough.

As to the franchise in those places which were recognised as boroughs, it varied widely in accordance with tradition or the wishes of the inhabitants. The scot and lot franchise (scot meaning those who paid local dues and lot those who held some office in local government) meant a very wide—what one might almost call a democratic—franchise. It was enjoyed in some populous and important places, of which the most notable was Westminster. It also existed in some of the most trivial of rotten boroughs such as Gatton. Wallop franchise meant that the franchise could be exercised by any who could boil a pot of his own and did not have to get his meals in another man's house. On election day citizens could be seen cooking a pot in front of their own front door to prove their qualification. This also was a fairly democratic franchise. Burgage franchise meant the vote for anyone who had a freehold ownership of a piece of land in the borough by burgage tenure. It was often insisted that he should live there and he would sometimes keep a chimney standing over a house that was not usually inhabited as evidence that it was capable of habitation. At other places the qualification was even more restricted and more eccentric. In some boroughs there was the freeman—or close corporation—franchise. In many such the membership of the corporation tended to be confined to members of a few close families or of those who married into them. If the freeman saw fit, as he often did, to sell his vote, membership of a borough with freeman franchise could be a very valuable property.

Up till the Civil War the ministers had been the King's

ministers and Parliament had existed as a check on the ministers. With the defeat of Charles I and after the Restoration, it was possible for Parliament to demand that the ministers be its servants. As long as Charles II was on the throne, precisely where sovereignty resided was still in doubt. It was not until George I's time that the matter was definitely settled in Parliament's favour. So long as the monarchy was still in a measure a claimant to sovereignty, the Whigs as its main opponent could pose as the party of freedom. The Tories were the reactionaries.

With the Parliament's victory their roles changed. The Whigs were now very content with things as they were, so long as they had got the King whom they wanted and held all the power of patronage in their own hands. There was in the early years of the century little Whig suggestion of any reform of the Parliamentary system. Such suggestions in so far as they came at all, came from the Tory Shippen. Later in the century there were some half-hearted suggestions of reform but they were not very seriously pressed. In 1770 Chatham, pronouncing that the boroughs were 'the rotten part of the constitution', suggested that a third Member should be given to all the counties. Wilkes in 1776 proposed a more ambitious general redistribution of constituencies. The Duke of Richmond in 1780 advocated manhood suffrage. Pitt, when he came into office in 1783, made a number of suggestions for reform, but soon they were all forgotten in the general panic of the French Revolution.

So long as the House of Commons was fighting against the pretensions of the King it appeared as the champion of liberty. When it became all powerful itself, its title grew more suspect in the popular eye. It was not, nor did it pretend to be, in any sense a democratic body and when the controversy about Wilkes's election as the Member for Middlesex arose, instead of a battle between King and Parliament for the rights of the people, the people saw the King and Parliament united in their attack on popular rights. Defoe had already warned them at the beginning of the century. 'Thus, gentlemen, you have your duty laid before you, which it is hoped that you will think of; but if you continue to neglect it, you may expect to be treated according to the resentment of an injured nation, for Englishmen are no more to be slaves to Parliament than to Kings.'

With the passage of time, the coming of the Industrial Revolution and the shift of population, the distribution of constituencies became yet more ridiculous. By the end of the eighteenth century, with the growth of the new industrial towns, the theoretical case for a reform of the constituencies was overwhelming. In Tudor times the population was predominantly in the South and it was not in itself ridiculous that the Members should have come predominantly from the South. When industrialism brought into existence the great Northern factory towns it was absurd that they should have no representation, for it was among them that the most of the greatest social problems were to be found and they had no one to speak for them. Yet even apart from this grave defect there were very many incidental absurdities in the borough representation.

The boroughs were found mainly around the coast where in Tudor times the greater part of the population lived, and they were particularly numerous in Cornwall and the South-west. In the eighteenth century the House of Commons returned 489 Members from England, 24 from Wales and 45 from Scotland. Another 100 were added from Ireland after the Union. The Scottish and Welsh boroughs returned only one Member each and the English, of which there were 246, with the exception of five single-Member boroughs and the City of London which had four Members, all returned two Members. Of the borough Members 142 came from the South-west: 44 from Cornwall, 26 from Devonshire, 20 from Dorset, 18 from Somerset and 34 from Wiltshire. Add in the 26 Members from Hampshire, 9 from Berkshire and 60 from Surrey, Sussex and Kent, and 237 Members—nearly half the House—came from south of the Thames.

The forty-shilling franchise was uniform throughout all

county constituencies though naturally with the changing value of money forty shillings in the eighteenth century had a very different meaning from what it had in Henry VIII's time. The number of voters varied greatly from county to county. In Rutland in 1760 there were 609. In Yorkshire in 1741, 15,054 and in 1807, 23,007. Most county elections were unopposed. In 1747 there were only two contests—in Middlesex and Staffordshire; in 1760 three—Durham, Hertfordshire and Westmorland. The average county electorate seems, according to Namier, to have been about four thousand. Voting, when there was a vote, was of course open and the names recorded in a poll-book—which meant that dependent voters were reluctant to vote against the wishes of their master. The general control of landowners over their tenants was taken for granted and considered proper. They often rigged the votes by creating faggot voters—that is to say, by conferring a title to freehold land on someone for the period of the election on condition that he rendered it up again as soon as he had recorded his vote and the election was over.

In 1832 there were two different forces pressing for reform. There were the friends of democracy and equality, represented among intellectuals by such men as John Stuart Mill, and among the ordinary people by Radicals who in a few years' time were to become Chartists and to denounce the Reform Bill as a fraud which promised them much and had given them nothing. And there were the new middle-class capitalists of the Industrial Revolution who, in a spirit which Marx was a few years afterwards so well to understand and denounce, saw that there had been a shift of economic power and demanded a corresponding shift of political power to give recognition to it: they demanded in particular the proper representation of the new manufacturing towns of the North and Midlands, such as Leeds, Birmingham or Manchester. It was the second class which won the victory of 1832.

The Act of 1832 did not attempt to divide up the whole country into equal constituencies. All that it did was to disfranchise the most grossly rotten boroughs and to distribute their seats among the hitherto unrepresented new towns. It disfranchised 56 boroughs absolutely, and took away one of its two Members from 31 more, re-distributing their odd Members. Perhaps more important—it for the first time laid down definite and general rules for the franchise. In the counties it preserved the traditional qualifications of a forty-shilling freehold but also added new qualifications for the £10 copyholder, the £10 long leaseholder, the £50 short lease holder and the £50 occupier. In boroughs, freemen were still entitled to vote but it also introduced a uniform £10 occupation franchise. It established for the first time a register on which everyone entitled to vote would find his name in-scribed, instead of as previously, having to justify his right to vote viva voce before the returning officer. The effect of the changes was to increase the borough elec-torate by about 100,000. Voting power was put effectively into the hands of the middle classes.

The system of 1832 lasted until Palmerston's death in 1865. Then the Liberals in office thought that the time had come for a further extension of the franchise. They brought in a bill which Disraeli and the Conservatives were able to defeat because the Liberals themselves split over the question. Then a little unscrupulously the Con-servatives introduced a somewhat more sweeping bill themselves. It gave the franchise to the £10 lodger. It also extended it in rural areas, reducing the £10 qualification for leaseholders to £5 and adding a £12 rateable qualifica-tion. Yet at the end of it all even after the Reform Act of 1867 the four million residents in the largest towns only returned 34 Members out of 658 and two thirds of the constituencies were still south of the Wash. The effect of these changes was to give virtually universal suffrage to the town working man. Agricultural labourers and women were the only classes generally excluded. Five years later in 1872 vote by ballot was introduced. The ballot, one of the original demands of the Chartists, was only conceded by a measure which granted it for one year, and that annual grant had to be renewed every year up till the Reform Act of 1918. Not until then was it made definitive.

Once the first and second Reform Acts had been passed it was almost inevitable that there would before long be a third Reform Act. It might to some people be an issue of principle whether votes should be extended to women or whether, as has happened in our day, the voting age be changed from 21 to 18, but nobody could believe as a matter of principle that the vote should be given to urban workers but denied to rural workers; and if the extension was sooner or later inevitable it was an obvious temptation to any party in power to make it sooner with the hope that they might, if they made the concession, get the support of the new voters. It was the Liberals under Gladstone who decided to make the concession. In 1884 he brought in a Representation of the People Act which extended to the counties the householder and lodger franchise of the towns. The occupation of any land or tenement of a yearly value of £10 was a qualification for a vote. He also introduced a new 'service franchise' to benefit some who by accident were not included in the other categories. The effect of these was to extend the vote to the agricultural worker and to increase the electorate by some 40 per cent. As after the other Reform Acts, the reform, while not producing any immediately drastic change in the type of person elected to Parliament, did bring a change in electoral programmes as both parties saw the necessity for bidding for the new voters. Previously Government, in agricultural matters, had for the most part dealt only with the landlords, and the tenant was left to make what bargain he could with his landlord. Now Government began to concern itself with the direct demands of the agricultural workers, and suggestions for a redistribution which might put the ownership of property within the reach of the agricultural worker began to be heard. There was a cry for 'three acres and a cow'.

The passage of the 1885 Bill into law was not without its difficulties. The House of Lords quite sensibly refused to pass an act for the extension of the franchise unless it

was combined with one for the redistribution of constituencies. Before 1832 there had been no pretence of
equality of population between constituency and constituency. The first two Reform Acts were only concerned
to disfranchise the most grossly rotten of the boroughs and
to give votes to the new towns which were scandalously
unrepresented. The new Act, at the House of Lords' in-
sistence, adopted the principle of the equality of constituencies. The constituencies should be redistributed on
the principle of one seat for every 54,000 people. On this
principle boroughs with less than 15,000 inhabitants were
disfranchised and absorbed into the county to which they
belonged. Boroughs with between 15,000 and 50,000 inhabitants were allowed to return a single seat, and towns
of such population which had not previously been boroughs
were created such and given a seat. Towns with popula-
tions between 50,000 and 165,000 were given two
Members, towns of above 165,000 an extra Member for
every additional 50,000. Boroughs which had previously
returned two Members and were qualified by their population to retain them remained two-Member constituencies. Others were geographically carved up into single-
Member constituencies, as were the counties. The Universities of Oxford, Cambridge and Dublin and the City of
London returned their two Members. This Act for the redistribution of seats, which was accepted by the Lords,
passed in 1885.

The Act appeared to be in the logic of things and was
passed as a Reform Act for Great Britain, and accepted as
such without any very great excitement. But it contained or
rather perfected one great anomaly. As a result of the
emigration following the famine of the 1840s, the population as between England and Ireland had vastly changed
since the passage of the Act of Union. By the Act of
Union a hundred Members came to Westminster from
Ireland. Had seats been redistributed on a strict population basis Ireland by 1884 would only have been entitled
to some 50 or 60 seats. Yet Irish discontent was so rife that
it was generally agreed that it would be unwise thus

dramatically to reduce the Irish representation. As a result, Irish constituencies were much smaller than British constituencies and Ireland was allowed still to send 108 Members. The extension of the franchise had another effect in Ireland that had hardly been foreseen at the time that it was being passed. Debates were concerned with the consequence of giving the vote to the British agricultural worker. But at the same time the extension of the franchise in Ireland gave the vote to the Irish peasants who had been most vigorous in revolt against the landlords and who were the strongest opponents of the landed system and the Union. As a result, in the next election the Irish Nationalists under Parnell, who had previously been able to carry only some half of the Irish constituencies, were able to carry every seat south of the Boyne, except the two from Trinity College. Parnell could for the first time justly claim to speak for a united nation. This confronted Gladstone, the Prime Minister, with an entirely new situation. Up till now he had been justly able to say to the Irish demand for Home Rule that it would be time enough for England to consider such a concession when Ireland had proved by a decisive majority that she really wanted it. Confronted at last with such a majority Gladstone could argue that as a Liberal it was his duty to consider it.

The electoral arrangements of 1885 lasted for thirty years until the coming of the First World War. During that war large promises were made of the new world that was to be offered to the troops when they came home and it was therefore natural, if all else was to be brought under review, that they should bring under review also the electoral system and see whether the machinery that was to make these improvements was itself capable of improvement. A Conference met under Mr. Speaker Lowther, the Speaker of the day, to see what reforms should be recommended. For the most part, the recommendations, though important, were not surprising. It was decided that the time had come to go forward to full universal suffrage based simply on residence. Property qualifications were abolished. It was decided in every constituency to draw up a register every six months. Anyone who had resided in the constituency for six months was put on the register and entitled to vote. A shifting population had made necessary a redrawing of constituency boundaries. The number of University Members was increased. Members were given to the Scottish and Welsh universities and the Combined English—what are known as the Redbrick Universities— and to London and Belfast University. A new device was introduced by which every candidate on nomination was compelled to make a deposit of £150, and those who failed to poll an eighth of the votes forfeited their deposit. This was designed to discourage freak candidates. Critics of the excessive rigidity of party discipline objected to it. But by far the most important change was that, not content with universal suffrage for men, votes were given to all women over thirty whose husbands were on the local government electoral roll. It was obvious that the very arbitrary age limit would not be held for long and, once that was abolished, there would be more women than men on the register. As many troops were still overseas in the months immediately after the Armistice when the election of 1918 was held, absent voting by post was permitted to those who could not vote in person. The changes proposed by the all-party Speaker's Conference were implemented in the Representation of the People Act, 1918.

The electorate was multiplied by seven. Since the 1918 Act the constituencies, with the further shifting of population have been changed from time to time. Women had their voting age reduced from 30 to 21 in 1928 and recently, along with men, still further reduced from 21 to 18. The University constituencies were abolished in 1948. Before 1918 a man who held property in a variety of constituencies could have as many votes as his property entitled him to. The Conservatives defended this plural voting and the Liberals denounced it. By the Act of 1918 a compromise was reached by which a man could have two votes—for his residence and for his business premises— but not more, unless he was also qualified for a University vote. The business vote was abolished in 1948 and a voter now has only a single vote: 'one man, one vote'.

Two very interesting suggestions were canvassed between the wars more seriously than they have ever been before or since. The traditional English system of voting is that of the simple majority in single-Member constituencies, or what the Australians called 'first past the post': that is to say, whoever receives the most votes is elected irrespective of whether he has an absolute majority or not. Whatever the advantages of simplicity of this system, it is obviously open to criticism. So long as differences of opinion are fairly evenly spread out over the country—as to a large extent they are—a party which has the support of 51 per cent of the electorate might win every seat and a party which has the support of 49 per cent get none at all. No result quite as inequitable as that has, it is true, ever been recorded in Great Britain, but in far more elections than not the party which has gained the majority of seats has had only a minority of votes, (most constituencies fielding at least three candidates). In the 1951 election, owing to the large number of Labour seats with heavily concentrated majorities, a majority of Labour votes in the country as a whole nevertheless returned a House of Commons which had a majority of Conservative seats and supported a Conservative Government. Small parties—as, for instance, the Liberal party at the present time—suffer particularly under the present system, and though they poll some millions of votes throughout the nation, the Liberals are hardly able to return any Members at all. Therefore the suggestion was made before Mr. Speaker Lowther's Conference that a system of proportional representation or one of the alternative vote should be introduced.

Under proportional representation, which had been canvassed in the time of John Stuart Mill, the single-Member constituency would be abolished and instead the country divided into large multi-Member constituencies. To be elected it would be necessary for a candidate to obtain a quota of votes, the quota consisting of the total number of voters divided by the number of Members to be elected. Every voter would have a single, transferable vote. On the first counting, attention would only be paid to those to whom they had given their first preference. If a candidate had received sufficient of such first preferences to give him the required quota, he would be declared elected and his surplus of votes distributed in proportion on the next counting to those to whom the voters had given their second preference. This process of redistributing would be repeated again and again until the full number to be elected had all attained their quotas, and in a constituency of, say, six Members, six candidates had been elected in proportion to the preferences of the electors. Thus in a city in which 60 per cent of the voters were Conservative, 20 per cent Labour and 20 per cent Liberal, all evenly distributed: under the present system, if the city was divided into the present six single-Member constituencies, all six elected candidates would be Conservatives, whereas under proportional representation, there would be four Conservatives elected, one Labour and one Liberal Member.

Under the alternative-vote system, the single-Member constituency would be preserved but within it each elector would have a transferable vote. He gave his first vote, say, to the Conservative and if, at first counting the Conservative got a clear majority, he was elected. If on the other hand no one got a clear majority then the bottom candidate was eliminated and the second preference of his votes was distributed among the other candidates. Thus the anomaly by which a candidate is very often elected when he has received only a minority of the total votes and when there is good reason to think that, if only the others had been able to combine against him they could have defeated him, would be eliminated.

Both these proposals were included in the original bill presented to the House of Commons as a result of the report of the Speaker's Conference. The alternative vote was passed by the House of Commons. But there was no great public enthusiasm for the experiment and it was

thrown out by the Lords. People in general did not understand either the complexities or the necessity for the plan
and preferred the excitement of a horse race in which the
man who came first was declared the winner. Proportional
representation was thrown out in the Commons; in the
Lords it was suggested that it was indeed unsuitable for
rural constituencies, where there was a real personal tie
between the Member and his constituents, but that there
could be no harm in introducing it into the large cities
with several Members and where the majority of voters
did not know either the boundaries of their constituency
or the name of their Member. Instructions were given for
a schedule to be drawn up dividing the constituencies
which were and were not suitable for the experiment. The
trouble about it was that such a scheme, leaving the rural
constituencies as single-Member constituencies and amal-
gamating the urban constituencies, would have given a
great advantage to the Conservatives who usually are able
to hold the majority of seats in the country. But this scheme
again aroused little interest and in the end proportional
representation was preserved only in the University
constituencies. It had there the effect that a much larger
number of Members independent of any regular party
allegiance were returned, at least after the Act had also
extended the franchise there to B.A.s. Previous to the Act
the Universities had always been very safe Conservative
constituencies.

It is, then, only over a short span in its comparatively
recent history that Parliament has been in any sort of
sense a democratic institution. More than that, it may be
argued that the establishment of democracy has led to the
decline of Parliament. Spengler has said that Parliaments
inevitably decline with the extension of the franchise.
Spengler perhaps was too much of a determinist, but
J. A. Spender, noting a decline in the public esteem ac-
corded to Members of Parliament, dated that decline from
1890—that is to say, almost exactly the date at which
something approaching a universal male franchise was
first established. It is at the same period that Parnell com-

pelled the imposition of those restrictions on the freedom
of debate that have so much increased the power of the
executive at the expense of the back-bench member. If we
were to generalise from historical experience it would be
much more plausible to define Parliament as an essentially
aristocratic institution that only worked satisfactorily in an
aristocratic milieu than as a naturally democratic institution.

IX

PARLIAMENT AND THE CROWN

As we have said, it is more than two and a half centuries since the monarch refused the royal assent to a bill that had passed through Parliament or since ministers have been in any real sense the Sovereign's personal ministers rather than the ministers of Parliament. Even when in the middle of the eighteenth century George III attempted to make a certain bid for personal power, he did it not by attacking Parliament from outside but by building up for himself within Parliament a body of King's Friends devoted to his interest. Nevertheless apart from the social influence of the monarch which has been enormous but with which we are not here concerned, his political influence has not been negligible. Parliament, and the King through Parliament, were sovereign not only of the United Kingdom but of His Majesty's Dominions beyond the seas. In the first British Empire the authority of the Declaratory Act specifically asserted the authority of the King in Parliament over the American territories. That claim could not be maintained but it was reiterated over the second British Empire. It was exercised over the colonies and over such countries as India. Over the Dominions—the countries to which self-government was granted—it became with time increasingly no more than a theoretical claim. By the Statute of Westminster of 1931 Parliament's claim to legislate for the Dominions was explicitly repudiated, but it was still imagined that the common acceptance of the crown was the one indissoluble link which kept the Commonwealth together. So much was this so that when the Irish declared their Republic in 1949 it was generally thought both in Ireland and throughout the Commonwealth that Ireland had automatically excluded herself from the Commonwealth. It was only later, with India's declaration of her Republic, that it was decided that a country could be a Republic and still remain a member of the Commonwealth.

It is perhaps worth enumerating the occasions over the last century when the Sovereign has been able to play an effective part in policy. At the beginning of the nineteenth century George III's influence was still strong enough to prevent the passage of measures of Catholic relief. William IV was still strong enough to dismiss Melbourne in 1834, and Victoria in the early years of her reign was able to refuse Peel's demand that he appoint his own Ladies of the Bedchamber and to prevent him from forming an administration so long as he insisted on that demand. Victoria was able to force Palmerston's resignation from the Foreign Secretaryship in Lord John Russell's administration, but throughout the rest of her reign, much as she liked to interfere in foreign affairs, she had to reconcile herself to the fact that the day had passed when it was possible for a monarch to have an independent foreign policy, and to confine her lust for power to the appalling ill-treatment of her own children. She often tried to exclude from Cabinets ministers whom she disliked, though usually without success. As long as Melbourne was alive she intrigued in favour of the Liberals and after his death in favour of the Conservatives. She opposed Irish Home Rule, writing to Goschen, 'I appeal to you and to all moderate, loyal and really patriotic men who have the safety and well-being of the Empire and the Throne at heart and who wish to save them from destruction with which, if the Government again fall into the hands of Mr. Gladstone, they would be threatened, to rise above party and to be true patriots.'

Even in modern times it has not been true that the monarch's role is purely decorative and his influence merely social, though Edward VII's part in bringing about the Entente Cordiale with France has probably been exaggerated. 'He never made an important suggestion of any sort on large questions of policy,' wrote Balfour. In the years before the First World War certain Conservatives suggested that the King should refuse his consent to the Home Rule Bill but George V very sensibly refused to entertain such folly. In 1923 when Bonar Law resigned and was too ill to give advice about his successor it was George V's personal decision which preferred Baldwin to Curzon. He resisted considerable pressure that he should attempt to bring about a coalition between Baldwin and Asquith rather than accept the first Labour Government in the next year. It is said that his was the influence which caused Macdonald to form a National Government in 1931. At the time of the crisis over the Abdication there was a little talk about a King's party, but it amounted to nothing and was hardly serious. In 1940 when Chamberlain fell it was at least generally thought that George VI would have liked Halifax to be his successor. If that was his wish, he was frustrated. Circumstances and public opinion compelled him to turn to Churchill. Twice Queen Elizabeth has had the difficult task of selecting a Conservative Prime Minister when the selection was by no means clear—once when Eden resigned and she sent for Mr. Macmillan, again when Mr. Macmillan resigned and she sent for Sir Alec Douglas-Home. She took in each case extensive advice and followed it, but the part of the monarch was by no means ritual.

X

THE FUTURE OF SOVEREIGNTY

1

The Threat of Disorder

Such is the parliamentary system. Whether it gives us democracy is largely a matter of semantics. Obviously it does not give us government by the direct will of the people. Referenda are not in our general tradition and have been in recent controversies most specifically repudiated. It is arguable that it gives us on the whole Government by consent of the people. What the people mainly want from the Government is peace and order and prosperity and a certain possibility of getting a change of masters, even if it is only a change of names, when they want to relieve their feelings. Freedom in this sense the system on the whole has given us and, whatever the deficiencies of the machinery of election, very few people would think it wise to abolish it.

Yet the system is at the moment threatened from three directions. The first two threats are of a kind with one another. The first challenge is the challenge of disorder. In one sense all authority is based on force. Parliament makes the law and the courts have to enforce it. But the extent to which force can be effectively used is very limited. Authority must also be based on consent. The policeman can step in to apprehend the individual law-breaker but he can only do so if the great majority of citizens obey the law willingly and without constraint. An authority can only be effective if it has prestige, if people obey it because they accept its authority and take that authority for granted. For this reason the proceedings of Parliament have rightly been enriched with a certain pageantry and ritual and for the same reason, if Members of Parliament wish to retain their authority, they must be careful to be seen behaving in a manner more decorous than the common man. In recent months there have been a depressing number of acts of violence and disorder in the chamber. No purpose would be served by recording the details of these disturbances which are at the moment in the public mind, for the particular incidents will certainly be forgotten by the time that these lines appear. But it is very important that these acts of disorder should prove to be but a passing phase from which the House, having let off its steam, is able to return to its traditional decorum. Disorder in the Commons is no new phenomenon. Whether the modern House has more of it than was seen during the Irish troubles of the 1880s who shall say? But certainly the world is at the moment in a very violent state. There is no more violence in this than in other countries. But there is violence—violence in our streets—and if Parliament's prestige is to survive it is most important that Members should not allow those habits of violence to spread from the streets into the chamber.

The second challenge is of a somewhat similar type. According to the theory of the Constitution, Parliament is sovereign. Without at the moment going into the question how far real authority rests with the Cabinet rather than with Parliament, it yet remains true that Parliament is legally sovereign. In fact the decisions both of the Cabinet and of Parliament are to a considerable extent influenced by the various pressures that are brought to bear on them. In particular it was proved in the early months of 1972 that the National Union of Mineworkers were able by striking and picketing to bring such pressure to bear on the Government and public that the Government had virtually to surrender to them and to grant to them concessions much more generous than it had ever intended or than it had thought in any way wise or deserved. Can such threats be repeated? Will they be repeated? Are we in sight of a brave new world where, whatever the nominal authority of Parliament or Cabinet, we will live in fact under a syndicalist domination? At the moment the Government has shown itself ready to meet the challenge. It sometimes wins its victories, sometimes it has to withdraw. At the moment of writing the final issue is still uncertain and would be necessarily uncertain at any moment of writing. The issue is unlikely to be one of clear-cut victory or of total surrender.

2

The European Community

The third challenge to Parliament is of a different kind. That issue has been presented by our attempt to enter the European Community. The controversy has revealed such deep divisions within both the political parties that it is not impossible that it will destroy the party system as we at present know it, and bring about a total rearrangement of parties. Doubtless, if Westminster survives at all, we shall in the end return to some sort of two-party system—our very architecture dictates it. But we may very well have to go through a period of floating groups and shifting combinations before the new parties form themselves, similar to the disorganised period through which the country went after the Repeal of the Corn Laws, before the subsequent Liberal and Conservative parties formed themselves under Gladstone and Disraeli. When first the issue of entry was presented to the House both the parties found themselves divided. Mr. Heath might have been expected to employ a three-line Whip to carry through his policy. The Opposition might more naturally have left things to a free vote. As a normal rule Oppositions are more ready to allow free votes than Governments for the obvious reason that it is essential for the Government, if it is to survive, that it win, while to the Opposition, ex-pecting to be defeated in any event, it is of secondary importance by what exact majority it is defeated. However on this occasion Mr. Wilson, anxious to preserve an appearance of unity for his party in which the Trade Unionists had come out in strong opposition to entry, put on a three-line Whip while Mr. Heath, judging that there were more pro-Market Members in the Labour party than there were anti-Market Members among the Conservatives, decided that he could leave the matter to a free vote. His courage proved well justified and he won a comfortable majority of 112. Mr. Wilson's hope that a three-line Whip would preserve his party's formal unity was frustrated. On later votes majorities have been narrower but it was soon evident that, as far as the House of Commons was concerned, Mr. Heath would be successful in taking the country into the Market and that he would not accede to the Opposition's demands for either a referendum or an election on the matter. Whatever may be the custom of other nations, there was no great reason why Mr. Heath should have acceded to the demand for a referendum here. The issue was only a little confused by Mr. Heath's rash promise that he would not take the country in without the 'full-hearted consent of Parliament and the people'. If the decision was to be taken by Parliament alone it was not easy to see what the words 'and the people' meant.

However that may be, it is certain that the clearest and most formidable challenge to Mr. Heath was that of those who, like Sir Derek Walker-Smith, claimed that acceptance of the conditions of the Treaty of Rome and the Brussels agreements would mean a surrender of British sovereignty. Whether such a surrender is or is not desirable it is no part of this book to argue. For what it is worth, the present author happens to be a supporter of acceptance of the Treaty of Rome. But that that acceptance does involve a surrender of sovereignty is beyond argument. Once the principle of entry was accepted it was to be decided whether there should be a series of bills spelling out in detail all the conditions which the Government was accepting or whether, as was done, all should be included in a single bill. The Government chose the latter course of a single short bill in Clause 2 of which we undertook the obligation to accept all provisions of the Treaty of Rome and the rulings of the Commission, whether regulations now existing (as on agricultural prices), or any that might in future be made. It gives the force of law in the United Kingdom to present and future Community law. All future regulations under the Treaties are to be given legal effect 'without further enactment'. It was natural enough that the Opposition should protest against the adoption of a guillotine procedure in order to carry such legislation through the House but, as in all protests by Oppositions against guillotine arrangements, these procedural protests were somewhat synthetic. They were not the real issue.

Supporters of entry argue with much cogency that in none of the six countries that have entered the Community has there ever been any suggestion of again leaving it. Opponents reply with equal cogency that, with their written constitutions, these countries have never given to their parliaments the absolute authority and sovereignty of British tradition. The immensity of the change, however, is beyond serious argument. There are those who argue that the changes will not in practice much effect the life of the ordinary citizen. This is clearly not so. We have already had to change the coins in our pockets and whether important or not, that is a change of habit that it is impossible not to notice. We are committed to policies of monetary unity which will forbid us to change our exchange rates against other member-countries.

It is certain that, as things go forward, either the Community will fail of its full effect and become little more than a friendly debating society after the manner of the Strasbourg Council of Europe, or else it will very radically change our whole traditional form of life. It is true, of course, that absolute national sovereignty is in the modern world something of a legal fiction. Quite apart from the demands of the European Community, we are already committed to a number of international bodies each involving limitations to our absolute sovereignty. To begin with, there is the United Nations, carrying with it such obligations as to refrain from aggressive war or to respect the Declaration of Human Rights. There is the International Monetary Fund. Then there are such smaller bodies as N.A.T.O. and W.E.U. and the Council of Europe, to which Parliament sends its British representatives.

It is argued that these bodies do not demand an abrogation of national sovereignty for two reasons. First they are not mandatory and the nations can only be committed to action if their recommendations are accepted by the ministers of the Government and approved by Parliament. Secondly we are told that our membership of these bodies is not irrevocable. If we sign the Treaty of Rome we sign for ever. There is no possibility of escape from our commitment. We have, of course, before now entered into engagements that were intended to be permanent and irrevocable and for the possible revision of which there was no provision. The Act of Union with Ireland is a case in point. Yet when it proved necessary to repeal that act it proved possible, even though the difficulties were very considerable. So if we should enter the European Community and if some future Parliament should wish to withdraw us from it, they would doubtless be guilty of a breach of faith if they did so, but there would be no constitutional provision to prevent them, at any rate until a European army, which could coerce us, had been created. The practical difficulties would be greatly increased the longer such a withdrawal was delayed and the more completely our economy was integrated with that of the European countries.

It is true that for the moment we are committed not merely to a European authority but to the authority of European bureaucrats. Whatever general suggestions about a democratically elected European Parliament may have been made, such a Parliament is not immediately in prospect. Nor can we immediately imagine a situation in which constituents in Yorkshire would be as willing to elect a man from Italy to represent them in a European Parliament as they might be to elect a man from Devonshire to represent them in the Parliament at Westminster.

Such developments may be in the logic of things. It is indeed in the logic of things that if we have a European Government we should have a European Parliament, but they are for the future. They are not immediate possibilities. In any event, they are not an answer to our problem in this book. We may live to see a European Government and that Government in every way better and at least as democratic as the British Government with which we have been so long familiar. But it will be a different government; and a Parliament which embodies the customs of other European countries as well as our own will necessarily be a different sort of Parliament from the Parliament of Westminster. The opponents of our entry are of two sorts. There are the obstinate nationalists who object to decisions over our lives being taken by foreigners. There are the champions of traditional Parliamentary sovereignty who object to our submission to a fixed and written constitution. Sovereignty at Brussels or Paris, at Luxembourg or Strasbourg, is a different thing from sovereignty at Westminster, and to the loss of that traditional sovereignty, for better or worse, we seem committed.

BIBLIOGRAPHY

Allen, A. J., *The English Voter*, 1964
Allen, C. K., *Law and Orders*, 3rd edition, 1965
  Law in the making, 6th edition, 1958
Amery, L. S., *Thoughts on the Constitution*, 2nd edition, 1953
Anderson, Sir John (Lord Waverley), *The Machinery of Government*, Romanes Lecture, 1946
Bagehot, Walter, *The English Constitution*, World's Classics, 1949
  The English Constitution, with an Introduction by R. H. S. Crossman, Fontana, 1963
Bailey, Sydney D, *British Parliamentary Democracy*, 1959
Bassett, R., *The Essentials of Parliamentary Democracy*, 2nd edition, 1964
Beer, S. H., *Modern British Politics*, 1965
  Treasury Control, 2nd edition, 1957
Belloc, Hilaire, and Chesterton, C., *The Party System*, 1913
Berkeley, Humphry, *The Power of the Prime Minister*, 1968
Bevins, Reginald, *The Greasy Pole*, 1965
Bonham, John, *The Middle-Class Vote*, 1954
Bradshaw, Kenneth, and Pring, David, *Parliament and Congress*, 1972
Bridges, Sir Edward, *The Treasury*, 1964
Brittan, Samuel, *The Treasury Under the Tories, 1951–1964*, 1964
Bromhead, P. A., *The House of Lords and Contemporary Politics*, 1958
Brown, W. J., *Everybody's Guide to Parliament*, 2nd edition, 1946
Bryce, Lord, *Modern Democracies*, 2 vols., 1921
Butt, Ronald, *The Power of Parliament*, 2nd edition, 1969
Campion, Lord, and others, *British Government Since 1918*, 1950
  Parliament, A Survey, 1952
Chester, D. N., and Bowring N., *Questions in Parliament*, 1962
Crick, Bernard, *The Reform of Parliament*, 1964
Cripps, Sir Stafford, and others, *Problems of a Socialist Government*, 1953

Dicey, A. V., *The Law of the Constitution*, 1885

Duverger, M., *Political Parties*, 1969

Ensor, R. C. K., *England 1870–1914*, 1936

Fairlie, Henry, *The Life of Politics*, 1968

Galbraith, J. K., *The Liberal Hour*, 1960

Gilmour, Ian, *The Body Politic*, 1969

Glass, S. T., *The Responsible Society*, 1966

Gordon, Strathearn, *Our Parliament*, 6th edition, 1964

Greaves, H. R. C., *The British Constitution*, 3rd edition, 1955
    The Civil Service in the Changing State, 1947

Grimond, Jo, *The Liberal Challenge*, 1963
    The Liberal Future, 1959

Guttsman, W. K., *The British Political Élite*, 1963

Haldane, R. B., *An Autobiography*, 1929

Halévy, Elie, *A History of the English People in the Nineteenth
    Century*, 6 vols, 1924–1951

Hankey, Lord, *Diplomacy by Conference*, 1946
    The Science and Art of Government, Romanes Lecture, 1951

Hanson, A. H., *Parliament and Public Ownership*, 1961

Hanson, A. H., and Wiseman, H. V., *Parliament at Work*,
    1962

Harvey, J., and Bather, L., *The British Constitution*, 1963

Herbert, A. P., *The Point of Parliament*, 1946

Hewart, Lord, *The New Despotism*, 1929

Hill, A., and Wichelow, A., *What's Wrong With Parliament?*,
    1964

Hughes, Emrys, *Parliament and Mumbo-Jumbo*, 1966

Hunter, Leslie, *The Road to Brighton Pier*, 1959

James, R. R., *An Introduction to the House of Commons*, 1961

Jenkins, Roy, *Mr. Balfour's Poodle*, 1954

Jennings, Sir Ivor, *The British Constitution*, 3rd edition, 1950
    Cabinet Government, 3rd edition, 1959
    The Law and the Constitution, 5th edition, 1959
    Parliament, 2nd edition, 1957
    Parliament Must Be Reformed, 1941
    Party Politics; Vol. 1, *Appeal to the People*, 1960; Vol. 2,
    The Growth of Parties, 1961; Vol. 3, *The Stuff of Politics*,
    1962

Jouvenel, Bertrand de, *Power*, 1948
    Sovereignty, 1957

Keeton, G. W., *The Passing of Parliament*, 1952
    Trial by Tribunal, 1960

Kersell, J. E., *Parliamentary Supervision of Delegated Legislation*, 1960

Keynes, J. M., *The General Theory of Employment, Interest and Money*, 1936

Laski, Harold J., *Parliamentary Government in England*, 1938
Reflections on the Constitution, 1951

Laundy, Philip, *The Office of Speaker*, 1964

Low, Sydney, *The Governance of England*, 1904

Lowell, A. L., *The Government of England*, 2 vols., 1908

McDowell, R. B., *British Conservativism, 1832–1914*, 1952

McKenzie, Kenneth, *The English Parliament*, 1950

McKenzie, Robert, *British Political Parties*, 2nd edition, 1963

Martin, Kingsley, *The Crown and the Establishment*, 1962

Miller, Edward, *The Origins of Parliament*, 1960

Monck, Bosworth, *How the Civil Service Works*, 1952

Moodie, G. C., *The Government of Great Britain*, 1964

Morrison, Herbert, *Government and Parliament*, 3rd edition, 1964

Muir, Ramsay, *How Britain is Governed*, 1930

Namier, L. B., *England in the Age of the American Revolution*, 1930
The Structure of Politics at the Accession of George III, 2nd edition, 1957

Neale, J. E., *The Elizabethan House of Commons*, 1949

Nicholson, Max, *The System*, 1967

Nicolson, Nigel, *People in Parliament*, 1958

Notestein, Wallace, *The Winning of the Initiative by the House of Commons*, Raleigh Lecture, 1924

Ogg, David, *England in the Reigns of James I and William III*, 1955

Ostrogorski, M. Y., *Democracy and the Organisation of Political Parties*, 2 vols, 1902

Pares, Richard, *King George III and the Politicians*, 1953

Plumb, J. H., *The Growth of Political Stability in England, 1675–1725*, 1967

Powell, Enoch, *A New Look at Medicine and Politics*, 1966

Raymond, John, *The Baldwin Age*, 1960

Stewart, J. D., *British Pressure Groups*, 1958

Taylor, A. J. P., *English History, 1914–1945*, 1965

Thomas, Hugh, ed, *The Establishment*, 1959

Thomas, P. D. G., *The House of Commons in the Eighteenth Century*, 1971

Turberville, A. S., *The House of Lords in the Age of Reform, 1784–1837*, 1958
Utley, T. E., *Occasion for Ombudsman*, 1961
Watkins, Alan, *The Liberal Dilemma*, 1966
Young, Roland, *The British Parliament*, 1962

INDEX

187